C000244361

JAMIE THOM

A TIME WITH LEOPARDS

A TIME WITH LEOPARDS

DALE HANCOCK

SWAN HILL PRESS

PREVIOUS SPREAD: PHOTOGRAPH BY NILS KURE

JAMES RAWDON

To the memory of my grandmothers:

Sheila Maud Rawlins and Anna Petronella Hancock

FIRST PUBLISHED IN THE UK IN 2000 BY SWAN HILL PRESS, AN IMPRINT OF AIRLIFE PUBLISHING LTD

BRITISH LIBRARY CATALOGUING-IN-PUBLICATION DATA
A CATALOGUE RECORD FOR THIS BOOK IS AVAILABLE FROM THE BRITISH LIBRARY

ISBN 1-84037-194-3

DESIGN AND PRODUCTION MANAGEMENT BY: HEATHER DITTMAR
EDITING BY: PETER BORCHERT AND BRENDA BRICKMAN
REPRODUCTION BY: HIRT & CARTER, CAPE TOWN
COLOUR RETOUCHING BY: WILLIE WIEGHARD, CAPE TOWN
PRINTED AND BOUND BY: TIEN WAH PRESS, SINGAPORE

AN IMPRINT OF AIRLIFE PUBLISHING LTD
101 LONGDEN ROAD
SHREWSBURY SY3 9EB ENGLAND
E-MAIL airlife@airlifebooks.com
WEBSITE www.airlifebooks.com

PETER CHADWICK

Contents

GRAHAM MITCHELL-INNES

Acknowledgements

There are a number of people whom I would like to thank. Firstly I must express my deep gratitude to the contributing photographers, many of whom have been very patient in waiting for the book to develop and travel through a number of potential publishers before reaching its final home with Black Eagle Publishers, three long years after it all started. For me, as with all the illustrated books I see and read, it is the images portrayed within that make it all work. I believe that the photographs appearing in this book are truly outstanding, and I thank you all for allowing me to use them.

As the short biographies on pages 130 and 131 attest, many of the photographers involved, all past and present rangers from Mala Mala, have impressive reputations and records as either professional or amateur photographers. I am very fortunate to have had such talent to draw from. While Kim and I were concentrating on filming the television documentary, it was the rangers who were covering the same or similar events with our or other leopards, using the sister and older art form that is stills photography. Whilst the images capture some unique and intimate moments of animal behaviour, they at the same time also manage to involve all the elements of a work of art: good composition, beautiful light and most importantly, capturing an event at the moment of greatest potential. All honour is your due.

Others whom I must thank are, of course, Kim and Annette Wolhuter for their support throughout; from the conception of the book and over the many years it took to bring to fruition. Kim, thank you for the friendship and for making the experience of the two years enclosed within these pages such fun, and for your editorial guidance. It also must be noted that the records shown in all the tables within each chapter are from Kim's detailed records kept each day while working on the film.

I must thank Nils Kure, ranger at Mala Mala from before we started work on *Beauty and the Beasts* in March 1993, and now manager of the elite Main Camp. Apart from his many pictures, Nils has kindly allowed me to quote from his own, unpublished writings of great insight. Also, Nils was instrumental in keeping some of Mala Mala's earliest records of leopard territories, which include whom was related to whom, from the early years of the 1990s, giving us a detailed image and understanding of many of our present-day characters' family trees. Nils, thank you for your help with the maps and for checking the accuracy of the lesser known territories indicated.

I would also like to thank wildlife film producer Richard Goss for employing both Kim and me to make the documentary *Beauty and the Beasts,* and thereby giving us these two years of invaluable memories living with our leopards. And then, similarly, the Rattrays, Michael and Norma, for permitting all of us access to their beautiful property. This has truly become a home from home. Many thanks.

I would like to pay tribute to David Evans of Mala Mala's Durban office for his enthusiasm for the project and all the staff of the three Mala Mala camps: the rangers, trackers, receptionists, caterers and all backroom and kitchen staff who have given us of their time, assistance and friendship so unconditionally.

From Black Eagle Publishers and Wild Dog Press, both Peter Borchert and Nick Pryke respectively must receive special thanks for recognising the potential of this book a little over a year ago, and for your guidance and efforts in finally making it happen. My thanks and gratitude to you encompasses all of your staff, especially Brenda Brickman, Shelley Prince, Heather Dittmar, Gillian Black, Alison Kreuiter, Linda Spinazzè, Simon Espley, and of course your families for shouldering some communications at home over the odd holiday or weekend. It has been a good experience.

Thank you all.

Dale Anson Hancock
Mala Mala Game Reserve,
April, 2000

Foreword

It is a great pleasure and privilege for me to write this foreword to *A Time With Leopards*. This book was made possible by National Geographic commissioning the filming of the life and behaviour patterns of one of Mala Mala Game Reserve's most exciting assets, namely the leopards. Dale Hancock's ability to photograph whilst simultaneously, through his writings, record accurate statistics about his subject makes this book extremely interesting for both animal lovers and scientists alike.

Dale has been associated with the Mala Mala Game Reserve since 1993 when he joined Kim Wolhuter to begin filming *Beauty and the Beasts – A Leopard's Story*, which will surely go down in history as one of the finest wildlife videos ever produced. Dale's obvious passion for leopards is clearly demonstrated in this written account, which encompasses the animals and their surroundings in a sensitive, albeit often tragic dimension that is interspersed with some of the more comical aspects of Africa's wildlife.

This work was supported by the conscientious and motivated team, which was an integral part of the success of the film production, and it is delightful that their passion is more than aptly portrayed in this finely presented record. The team effort also includes the unselfish contribution made by the Mala Mala rangers; a number of their photographic records have been included in *A Time With Leopards*, adding significantly to the impact of the book.

I am delighted that one of Africa's jewels – Mala Mala – has been the platform on which this production has been staged. It says a lot for our environmental management practices and a lot for our neighbours, the famous Kruger National Park. It says even more for the actors – those leopards that continue to enthrall the multitude of visitors who travel long distances to our continent to witness, first hand, the magic of Africa.

Michael L. P. Rattray

PHOTOGRAPH: NILS KURE

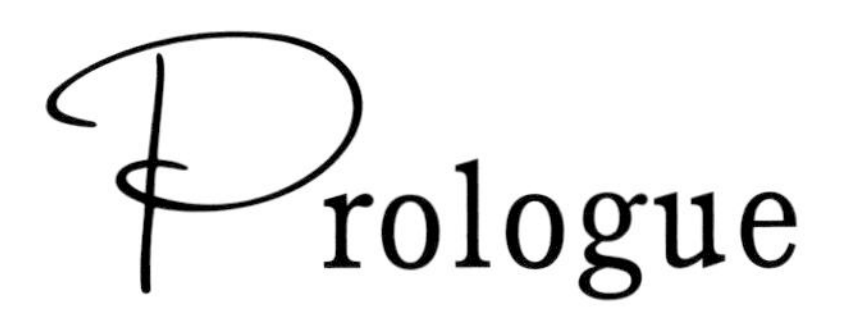

Prologue

Dawn in the Lowveld is unmistakable. Almost before the horizon begins to lighten at the approach of the coming day, the Mozambique nightjars call an end to the long hours of darkness. At first they are unchallenged, but soon a chorus of other birds such as the raucous crested francolins, join in with gusto. All around us the bush wakes.

Lying not five metres away, fast asleep on the crest of an anthill topped with golden grass bending gently to the first morning breeze, is the subject of our attentions, not only for the previous night, but for the past 15 months – a female leopard. She is stunningly beautiful. The first rays of light filter through the mosaic of marula trees to fall on her dappled flanks, emphasizing their colour and form. Overhead, there is a burst of one of summer's most characteristic sounds, the distinctively rich, penetrating call of the woodland kingfisher. Reluctantly the leopard opens her eyes in response. She yawns three times in brief succession and then rolls onto her belly to survey her surroundings.

From the new season's long grass entangled with the stems of impenetrable *Strychnos* trees, another lithe form emerges. And then another follows, just as sleek. The family is complete.

One of the nearly fully grown cubs approaches her recently roused mother and attempts the typical ritual greeting that has accompanied almost every morning since her birth. She brushes along her parent's flank, butting the adult female as she glides past. The cub collapses forward, rolling her neck and shoulders on the ground before returning to her mother to repeat the sequence. Much to her surprise, this time she is met not with the expected maternal lick and grooming, but with the intimidating snarl usually reserved for their greatest enemies, the hyaenas. With teeth fully bared in unmistakable disapproval, the mother leopard eases out a long, controlled hiss at her daughter. The message is clear: it is time for the cub and her sister to move on.

But they will not have to leave immediately. This morning was only the first of many rebuffs to come before the youngsters would eventually accept the inevitable and move away in search of their own territories, and to raise their own cubs – if they can. It also signals that we are nearing the end of our time with them, when we, too, will have to say goodbye to the cubs that have become our good friends. And shortly thereafter, as our project draws to a close, we will have to bid farewell to our greatest friend of all, their mother.

Living with 'our' leopards has been a very productive and entertaining period. It has been a privileged time that we shall surely remember forever ...

PHOTOGRAPH: CHRIS DAPHNE

CHAPTER ONE

Beginnings

PETER CHADWICK

It ought to be realized that lion, leopard,
wild dog, jackal and other predatory creatures,
great and small, and whether of the earth,
air or water, have their full place in nature, just
as much as the animals on which
they are accustomed to prey, and are entitled
to equal respect.

Colonel James Stevenson-Hamilton
South African Eden

DALE HANCOCK

Tjellers relaxes, seemingly oblivious to her cub attacking her tail.

DALE HANCOCK

RICHARD DU TOIT

TOP *A female buffalo stares balefully at the camera. Two herds roam the Mala Mala property, each numbering several hundred individuals.*
ABOVE *Mating locusts on an acacia tree.*

It was with great enthusiasm that Kim Wolhuter and I teamed up in 1993 to film leopards. With the experience of two other international wildlife films to his credit, one in Botswana's Okavango Delta and the other on the Lüderitz coast of Namibia, Kim was accustomed to working in highly challenging environments. I was the relative newcomer, joining the project as lighting technician, sound recordist and assistant cameraman to Kim. The prospect of being able to learn more about the habits of leopards was very exciting. No longer would our sightings be mere fleeting glimpses of elusive cats – here was an opportunity for us to reveal their very secretive lives.

Kim and I had been commissioned by Richard Goss, who had been producing wildlife films in southern Africa since 1982, and already had a number of productions under his belt for the prestigious BBC Natural History Unit. Richard was based in White River, a small town perched at the edge of the Drakensberg Escarpment, and we were set to film down below in the Mpumalanga Lowveld, some 100 kilometres away. Our precise locality – the magnificent Mala Mala Game Reserve. And, notwithstanding early setbacks, it could not have been a better choice.

There are many other private reserves within the Sabi Sand Complex to the west and north of Mala Mala's boundaries, all of which offer leopard sightings. None, however, offers the predictability and reliability of encounters that Mala Mala does. Sprawled over more than 16 000 hectares, Mala Mala is much larger than any of the neighbouring private reserves and, set on both sides of the Sand River along 35 kilometres of its winding course, the property is most attractive to the area's game throughout the year. For example, the reserve is home to numerous resident lion prides, more than 30 leopards, a good number of white rhinos, and two herds of buffalo each comprising many hundred individuals. Several bull elephants as well as a number of herds also reside almost entirely on the property. Smaller game is prolific and, now that the boundary fences have been removed, there is a constant flow of animals to and from Mala Mala's vast eastern neighbour, the Kruger National Park.

In a typical two-day spell at any of Mala Mala's three camps (Main, Kirkman's, and Harry's) rangers can almost guarantee sightings of all of the Big Five – lion, leopard, elephant, rhino and buffalo – but most especially the leopard. A shy and solitary animal, with embossed black rosettes dappling a sleek, orange-brown coat, this extraordinarily elegant cat has always been one of the most sought after of Africa's wild animals – as much by the pioneer hunters of old, as by the game-viewing enthusiasts of today. The leopards at Mala Mala have become habituated to the presence of man and his accompanying machinery and probing lights. It is no doubt now far easier than it was in times gone by to spot, and indeed to follow this elusive cat.

For decades Mala Mala doggedly sent out their game-drive vehicles twice a day to track down leopards, and even as little as 10 years ago it was considered a great bonus to have sighted one. The lucky ranger and tracker to achieve this feat would ride high for days, if not weeks, on the esteem afforded them by the rare find.

Today, and on a single game drive, as many as 13 individuals – although more generally two or three – can be seen in the space of a few hours. I know of no other place

DALE HANCOCK

in the Lowveld where one can almost be assured of the nightly guttural sawing of a leopard's call. It has been established that the area surrounding the confluences of the Sabi and Sand rivers holds the highest density of leopards in the world, and Mala Mala is only a small distance north of this spot.

NILS KURE

TOP *A game drive at Mala Mala delivers a prized sighting for the guests – a leopard draped across the trunk of a fallen tree.* **ABOVE** *Mala Mala Main Camp reception area.*

Before Michael Rattray acquired the original and much smaller Mala Mala from his family in 1975, the reserve was essentially known only to a select few South Africans, mainly as a convenient getaway from their stress-filled lives in the big cities a few hours' drive to the west. Shortly after taking control of the reserve, Michael and his wife Norma undertook a drastic revamping and revitalization of Mala Mala. Accommodation was updated, two new camps were built (Harry's and Kirkman's), a new fleet of vehicles was purchased, and tariffs were raised to more appropriate levels. In short, a whole new course was set for what has become one of South Africa's most prestigious wildlife destinations for local and international tourists alike. In fact, on several occasions now, Mala Mala has been voted the best small hotel in the world.

Mala Mala has become a name synonymous with the highly marketable Big Five. Today, however, the Big Five at Mala Mala and the other Sabi Sand reserves have become the most sought after species by a very different 'hunter' – the ecotourist – and to be shot not with a weapon, but through the lens of a camera.

Interestingly, and as recently as five decades ago, Harry Kirkman (the man after whom the two newer Mala Mala camps are named) and his fellow compatriots in conservation at the time, used to shoot any and all lions they came across. In fact it was considered good management policy in those early days, even within the national

NILS KURE

RICHARD DU TOIT

TOP *A furry bundle of sleepy lion cubs, members of one of Mala Mala's numerous prides.*
ABOVE *With a gentleness belying the strength of her powerful jaws, a lioness mouths her cub.*

parks such as Kruger, to shoot not only lions, but leopards and wild dogs too. Although today such a policy would be unthinkable, the theory then was that it would help conserve some of the more vulnerable prey species, which at the time were thought to be rapidly depleting in number.

Kirkman was employed in 1927 as warden of the Transvaal Consolidated Land and Exploration Company (TCC), which then owned most of what is today known as the Sabi Sand Complex, and included the whole of what is now Mala Mala. The TCC was engaged in cattle ranching and had been battling with predation, specifically from lions, so it became Kirkman's job to eradicate them from the area.

Legend has it that Kirkman loved the wild. Nonetheless, he was obviously well suited to the task of resolving the lion problem. In six short years, he killed over 400 lions that strayed into his area from the adjacent Kruger National Park. Out-and-out war had been declared on lions in particular, and on all predators in general.

In time, though, and thanks to a few far-thinking individuals in a position to do something about the carnage, the cattle were removed from the area and wildlife was once again allowed to prosper unchecked. The man who led the way was Colonel James Stevenson-Hamilton, first warden of the Kruger National Park. Displaying foresight well ahead of his time, the doughty Scotsman realized the ineffectiveness of such predator control. Thankfully, he was successful in terminating the policy before such susceptible species as the wild dog were forced into local extinction.

Ever the articulate writer, Stevenson-Hamilton clearly set out his thinking in *South African Eden,* an enthralling account of his time in the Lowveld. 'As far back as 1904 I was assured that, unless all lions were shot, the game reserve could not exist for 3 years ... Nevertheless, after having observed conditions in the reserve most closely for 3 decades, I am convinced that Nature can, and will, maintain its own balance ... To my mind, one of the ideals is to find the answers to the multitude of unsolved mysteries of nature, scientific or otherwise, which can be sought and are to be found only in an area where all the indigenous species are permitted to follow their natural way of life ... in other words, how they were supposed to have lived before man became a factor in their lives.' And it is my opinion that today, at Mala Mala, the Rattrays have managed, with dedication, to achieve a level of this dream.

At first the idea of shooting a film on one of Africa's most secretive animals was an intimidating thought for both of us. Kim, the project cameraman and director-in-the-field, had been at Mala Mala for a number of months prior to the commencement of filming, finding his proverbial feet, so when I joined him at the reserve in March 1993 he had already picked out our stars to be.

My first night's work involved driving down south from Main Camp (where we had started off, before relocating to Harry's Camp), to film the chosen leopard at her lair. I was struck by the ease with which she accepted our presence and the intrusion on her privacy, especially with such young cubs so close at hand.

For three consecutive nights, just after dark, we watched as the cubs emerged to play. Hours would pass as they tumbled over rocks, tugging at their mother's tail and play-fighting. Then, quite suddenly, they would settle, and after suckling them briefly, she would leave them to hunt. This was where our troubles started.

Even though Mala Mala is home to so many leopards 'familiar' with man, to track down a single individual and remain with it night after night is no mean feat. The terrain is not the easiest to traverse, especially in the south of the reserve where we spent most of our time. Made up of six nearly equally sized farms, the property follows the route of the Sand River as it winds its way south past Harry's camp (our base for two years), and into the Kruger National Park. In this area, peppered with *dongas* (deep gullies caused by natural soil erosion) and dense riverine bush, we spent most of our first month repairing our vehicles as we discovered our limitations by trial and error.

I was expecting that the problem of constantly losing our subject – usually before the night's work had even begun – would be solved by the more experienced Kim, and was confident that a solution would be found. But after another month of being hampered by the dense vegetation and having little to show for our efforts we, together with our producer, Richard Goss, had to take serious stock of whether this production would ever reach completion. Only the approach of autumn and the expectation of improved visibility fuelled our hopes.

With the dry season on its way, we pushed on.

PIETER DROS

DALE HANCOCK

TOP *Roosting white helmet-shrikes.*
ABOVE *A wild dog pup and its toy – the tusk of a warthog.*

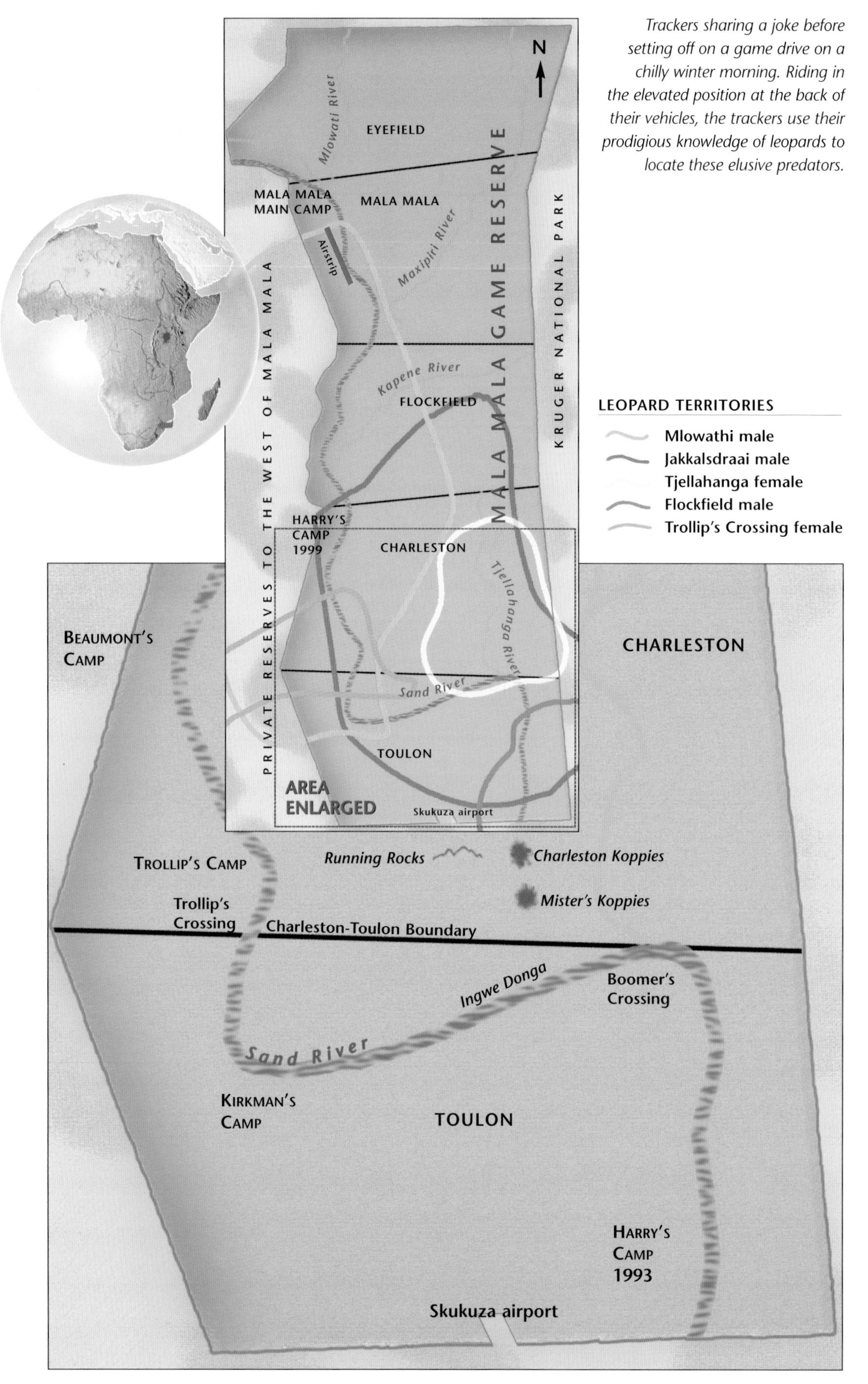

Trackers sharing a joke before setting off on a game drive on a chilly winter morning. Riding in the elevated position at the back of their vehicles, the trackers use their prodigious knowledge of leopards to locate these elusive predators.

RICHARD DU TOIT

CHRIS DAPHNE

CHAPTER TWO

Characters

NILS KURE

The leopard is an animal of great beauty – the perfect example of feline power and grace. Solitary, secretive and aloof, it is an unmatched predator and a powerful symbol of the wild places of the earth. To see a leopard moving through the African bush, or even lying motionless draped in the high branches of a tall tree, is a riveting experience.

Anthony Hall-Martin
Cats of Africa

A mother leopard is constantly on the move with her young offspring, relocating them time and again from one den to another. This strategy helps to minimise the risk of her cubs being located and killed by rival predators, particularly lions and hyaenas.

DALE HANCOCK

A black-backed jackal sniffs intently at a grass stalk, possibly checking for the scent of a rival. Jackals mate for life and vigorously defend their territories against potential invaders.

Our chosen subject was the Tjellahanga female. She was a good choice, particularly considering it was one more of circumstance than calculation. At the time, she was the only female on the property that was known to have two newborn cubs.

Also, autumn brought a thinning terrain, and with it we became more adept at following our 'stars', learning together with the cubs the extremities of their mother's territory, who their neighbours were and, of course, their enemies.

We had become privileged observers of the daily life of a leopard family, or 'rosette' of leopards as we liked to call them (much to the disdain of the rangers at Mala Mala). Perhaps because leopards are classified as solitary animals, there exists no collective noun for them, even though they occasionally occur in small groups. We coined 'rosette' after the embossed, spot-like patterns that make up a leopard's coat.

At first glance, and to the untrained eye, most leopards appear remarkably similar – initially it is even difficult to tell male from female (if no hind view is possible). And yet, as our familiarity with the Tjellahanga female grew, we became more and more convinced that we had been landed with the most attractive female leopard at Mala Mala. Of course, some of the staff on the property disputed this in honour of their personal favourites, but to us, Tjellers, as we soon nick-named her, was clearly the beauty of beauties.

Admittedly over time we encountered some adolescents, including one of Tjellers' own cubs, that were equally as beautiful, but we discounted them feeling that youth was definitely on their side. None of these other individuals was a settled, reproducing adult like Tjellers, and for an adult seven-year-old leopard with four litters to her name (and a grandmother to boot!), she was astonishingly attractive. A leopard can live up to about the age of 20, and Tjellers still had many prime years ahead of her. Our 'choice' could not have been better.

A little further north on the reserve we encountered another female with a single male cub. This was the Hogvaal female, and initially we thought it might be a good idea to double up on our resources by working with her and Tjellers, especially as all three cubs were of about the same age, and we could have intercut the footage if need be. In this way, when no interesting developments were taking place within the one family, we could drive over to the other and hopefully get something else on film before dawn.

However, after our first visit with the Hogvaal female we soon changed our minds. This female was fierce and definitely a force to be reckoned with! Without any provocation and when you least expected it, she would rush at you in a startling display of ferocity. One moment you could be sitting in the vehicle within metres of her and her cub, neither of them showing any signs of stress, and the next, the grass would explode with muscle, fur and claws hurtling towards you behind a wall of ivory-white teeth.

We learned that this usually placid female became extremely and erratically ferocious when she had a new litter of cubs. The rangers, of course, knew her only too well and were ready for her rush, but the guests, even if forewarned, were not. When the little Hogvaal 'bombshell' exploded from cover the guests would all rock back in unison like a mini Mexican Wave, the closest members of the group clearly terrified. Never really serious about her charge, she would always stop well short of the vehicle, do an about turn and head back, tail thrashing, to her bewildered cub who seemed not to understand what all the fuss was about. This obviously made for good viewing and a memorable experience for the guests, but it was hardly conducive to documenting the natural behaviour of leopards. Even if we tried reassuring her by backing off a distance, the Hogvaal female would still charge at the least expected moment, sometimes ages after our initial approach. It was never our purpose to cause her any undue stress, so we decided it would be for the best if we dedicated ourselves exclusively to Tjellers and her cubs.

DALE HANCOCK

Depsite our concerted efforts not to disturb our subjects, we were occasionally warned, in no uncertain terms, to keep a respectful distance.

Tjellers was far more placid. Even when she would clearly have preferred to be left alone, if only for just a few minutes, she would maintain her dignity, simply lifting her nose with a distinct air of superiority and slowly turning her head away. A clear, yet graceful snub that we were mostly too rude to take any notice of. One can understand and respect an essentially solitary individual wanting her own space and distance from us, but any misgivings about disturbing her were matched by our determination to document everything that a leopard was; and that meant sticking to her like glue until she learned to ignore us completely. As Tjellers was already well used to intruders after all the years she'd spent being viewed by guests, it did not take long to achieve this. Still, she occasionally tried to outwit us.

To begin with she would sneak off the road as we drove up behind her in the hope that we would pass by. In these instances we would pull up alongside the bush she was behind or hiding in and talk to her, leaning slightly from the vehicle down to her level to do so. Clearly unimpressed and with ears flat, she would spring from the bush and with a small grunt, trot off down the road again as if to show us she really had no intention of hiding and that it was merely a game to test how alert we were. Sometimes we would pretend not to have seen her and drive on past. Looking round when she was some 50 metres behind us, we would find her sitting up in full view of the world with a very contented look on her face – until we turned our vehicles and headed back in her direction. It was always a light-hearted play of wits to see who would be the day's victor.

NILS KURE

Tjellers would often hide from us, skulking off behind a bush and waiting for us to pass before reappearing. It was as if she was testing us to see how alert we were.

The decision to stick to filming only the one female and her cubs, albeit a forced one, proved to be a blessing in disguise. Many a time when we had settled down for the night with the thought that there was little chance of any activity worth filming, something unexpected would happen. All too often some incident would rouse us from slumber at the base of the tree in which Tjellers and her cubs were sleeping, in time to witness and record another

DALE HANCOCK

A white-faced owl, one of our many visitors during the long nights of filming Beauty and the Beasts.

NILS KURE

ABOVE *The cubs always took great interest in our clothing and if we were careless enough to leave any item unattended it was 'stolen' in a trice. Here a cap is the prize, but Four's favourite was undoubtedly Kim's balaclava.*
OPPOSITE *Some of our most pleasurable moments came from watching the cubs – insatiably curious and always playful.*

unique chapter in their lives. Had we been running between her and the Hogvaal female, we would have missed many interesting escapades, and probably only ended up duplicating what we had managed to record in the company of Tjellers and her family.

After spending some time with Tjellers we were surprised to note the marked personality differences between her two cubs: they were obviously born twins, only minutes apart; and both were females sired by the same father and brought up through many months of all the same trials and tribulations while following their mother. Yet, even from early in their development, the one cub showed a marked boldness of character, whilst the other seemed very reserved. Perhaps we might have found this more understandable if they were male and female, but they were not.

The more self-assured of the two was acutely aware of everything around her and, of course, this included us. If not for her mother's and sister's disapproval, she seemed almost content to adopt us as a part of her greater family. Never was an opportunity passed up to snatch a garment of clothing left hanging carelessly unguarded from a vehicle. Once in possession of such a play item she would parade around with it dangling from her mouth, sometimes tripping herself up with her not-entirely coordinated movements. Somehow I think she used to feel it gave her higher status than her more careful sister, and she would flaunt her unusual 'kill' in front of her sibling.

One of her greatest prizes, Kim's winter balaclava, was tirelessly carried about from early one morning, until we returned to find the family again that evening. Eventually, and I dare say reluctantly, she abandoned the cumbersome item in order to follow and keep up with her mother's brisk pace. (Kim couldn't have been happier at the opportunity of retrieving his balaclava as the cold winter bite along the Sand River came early on those particular evenings.) Her sister might have been impressed, her mother clearly was not, and no preferential treatment was afforded this little show-off!

While the cub offered us many hours of amusement at her antics, I am sure we provided her with just as much mutual entertainment. She would regularly investigate us at close quarters – and this of her own initiative, sometimes even stretching out a paw to try to touch us. Extend your hand to her and after a few cautionary glances back and forth from hand to face to check for any signs of aggression, she would be compelled to take up the offer. She was very gentle. Kim would offer her the upper surface of his hand and she would extend her claws just enough to lightly scratch his skin. But if he turned his hand over, so that the palm was facing up, she would completely retract her claws and pat at his hand with her paw, whisking it away as quickly as possible. No lingering clawing this time: she was not prepared to risk her paw being held captive in his hand.

PETER CHADWICK

NILS KURE

Tjellers and Stevie. We found that females and their newborn young spend surprisingly little time together – often the parent leopard would abandon her cubs for days before returning to suckle them.

Although relaxed, her more reserved sister preferred to watch these exploits from a safer distance. Any temptation to join in must have been tempered by a healthy respect for, or fear of these uninvited guests. Of the two of them I am sure the more timid was the more typical leopard – especially when it came to natural behaviour. The bolder was quite crazy! She was always the first to invite trouble. In the entire two years of filming, never did we find another leopard, adult or cub, that would approach and investigate us at close range just as a matter of curiosity, or in quite the same way. Sometimes she would spend hours preoccupied with us, while her sister busied herself with learning to be a leopard. As the cubs grew older both mother and the more typical youngster would move off, leaving the adventurer to the folly of her ways, and her own limited resources. More often than not she would realize too late that she had, yet again, been abandoned for the day.

DALE HANCOCK

Cubs soon learn to recognize the threat posed by hyaenas. Here a cub mimics its mother's threat display – from the safety of a fork in a tree.

From an early age no leopard will allow another to feed off a carcass while it is itself engaged in feeding. This particular cub, however, felt no threat to itself or its meal even if we were to film from a position opposite her, just inches from her kill. It was at times like these that we would love to have known just exactly what it was she considered us to be. We were not a threat, but neither were we family. On one occasion we were so amazed by her tolerance at our presence that we could not resist testing her by pulling at the carcass on which she was feeding. The most reaction we could muster from her was a hiss – a particular trait of hers that we learnt to recognize early on, when she was still a young cub, as more of a respectful recognition of our presence than a hostile threat to our person. A remarkable individual indeed.

Subsequent to our experiences with 'our' leopard cubs we were interested to note in Lex Hes' book, *Leopards of Londolozi*, how this difference in the characters

CHRIS DAPHNE

The bush of the South African Lowveld is ideal terrain for leopards. It is here that they are most at home, and at Mala Mala they are more numerous than anywhere else in the world.

DALE HANCOCK

Leopards mostly use rock overhangs and shallow caves in which to hide their young, but they are resourceful animals and in emergencies they will also resort to the shelter provided by hollow, fallen trees.

of leopard twins was not a unique observation. Quite the contrary, it was almost as if Lex was describing our own two cubs when he wrote: 'Both cubs were females, but it seemed that they had already developed individual characters. Sticknyawo was slightly smaller than her sister and far more relaxed with the Land Rovers. She was very inquisitive and not afraid to come right up to the vehicle to peer quizzically up at the people sitting in it, or to walk casually past, not more than a metre away. Her sister was much more reclusive, keeping her distance and not showing the same curiosity.'

One has to ask oneself if there is not something to this strange, coincidental parallel? How often does this total split in personalities occur? Is this yet another of Nature's impressive techniques of ensuring a species' survival? Man has come a long way in understanding the ways of the wild, and just recently in our history something of the essence of the leopard, but there is still so much we can and have to discover.

It has been said many times before how science should veer away, at all costs, from anything and everything emotive or anthropomorphic, when dealing with Nature. There is certainly much motivation for this point of view, but in our opinion it is also a hard-line and excessive attitude. Wild animals have emotion and characters just like domestic animals do. Granted, we humans all too often attach wrong interpretations to what other species might be feeling, or to their possible motives for doing what they do. But by the same token, we cannot be totally blinkered about basic emotions common to many species of higher intelligence, and that must include leopards.

Mala Mala has a policy that avoids giving animals character-depictive names; instead, location-specific 'labels' are chosen. With an operation of this size and reputation, and for immediate specifics on the sex and type of animal spotted and where to find it, the rangers need to be as brief as possible when calling in sightings. Certain of the animals, too, are known to be either relaxed (where they might still be in the same spot when you come charging over – 20 minutes later – from the other side of the reserve), and others will bolt at the mere presence of a vehicle. Hence the decision to name the animals according to the epicentre of their territory. For example, Tjellers, the Tjellahanga female, had been so-named many years before our arrival after the main river tributary that runs through the core of her territory.

But what of Tjellers' two cubs? Neither of them had names. Nor would they be given any until they were established, territorial adults, and then only if they remained on the Mala Mala property.

We had nearly a full two years still to spend with 'our' family, and clearly we could not continue referring to the two of them merely as the bold or the timid one. Something would have to be thought of. As documentists and dramatists, we believe that animals do have individual characters and are not against giving them indicative names.

Being film makers we like to develop a relationship with our characters as friends in the hope that this will eventually be carried through to our audience. As the cubs were just so cheeky (more than usual) we couldn't help but to try to give them names that would match their precociousness. Nothing too obvious or soppy, just something that had a cocky ring to it.

We enjoyed a very good working relationship with the Mala Mala staff and, lunch-time being our only hour spent in relaxation with them outside of work, much friendly banter was passed back and forth across the riverside table. Many topics were discussed with great enthusiasm, although most centred around things linked to our immediate situations and daily lives in the bush. The naming of our cubs was just one of these diversions. Knowing the policy of the reserve, we knew the rangers would baulk at the fact that we had even given the cubs names, let alone what we had chosen.

We decided on 'Two' and 'Four'. Indisputably, the names were unconventional; we thought they were perfect, particularly as nobody seemed to know quite what to make of them. Although the names may appear senseless, they were actually quite logical as well as descriptive. Every leopard has distinct whisker spots, like the human fingerprint, which are quite easy to recognize with a little practise. Ignoring all except the top rows above the whiskers, both cubs had three spots on the right-hand side of their faces, but on the left, the timid one had only two and the bolder one four. Quite simple and unmistakable. It was some time before we satisfied the rangers' curiosity as to the true motive behind our cubs' names. They were nonplussed and for the time being their confusion was something to be enjoyed.

NILS KURE

ABOVE AND BELOW *The dry winter season, when the bush is sparse and open, is often cited as the best game-viewing time. But many species such as the impala and giraffe drop their young in the green months of summer. Watching the engaging antics of newly born animals is always entertaining.*

The young of any species are always great fun to watch. Minutes, and even hours can pass without them noticing that their antics are being observed. It was thus a great temptation for us to spend as much time as possible with Two and Four in their first months, in preference to going off with their mother, fighting our way across *dongas* and through the nearly impenetrable bush. But we knew this was a cop-out, and that following Tjellers would invariably continue to produce a variety of new and interesting sequences to film. Although usually highly entertaining, sitting with the cubs held limited potential as far as useable footage was concerned before it fast became repetitive. Tjellers in any event already spent sufficient time with her two cubs, when not hunting, to satisfy our desire to be with them. Moreover, they were generally most active and fun to watch when with their mother.

We found Tjellers' activities peaked at three basic periods throughout each night. As long as she did not already have a kill, her night's hunting would commence at around sunset for a few hours, through until about 10 o'clock, when

PETER CHADWICK

DALE HANCOCK

DALE HANCOCK

she would rest up wherever she was. This would last until the small hours of morning (about one o'clock), when she would resume her prowling. If still unsuccessful, she would rest again for a few hours until just before first light, when she would try one last time to kill. This last period of hunting often ended up more diurnal than nocturnal, lasting as long as it was cool enough to move comfortably. In winter, if she was really determined to kill, this could last until almost midday. For instance, the film's climatic end kill in broad daylight was filmed at 11 o'clock in the morning. When her cubs were still very young she would return to them for these intermediary periods of rest to suckle them, but later would only return to them once every day or two, or when she had finally killed to call them to feed. We kept a record of Tjellers' kills – the number and the time of day or night.

After each successive meal had been polished off by Tjellers and her cubs, she would move the family unit to a new location within her territory before sleeping and eventually going off again to hunt alone. But on one of these trips, when the cubs were still quite small and vulnerable to predation by hyaenas if surprised by one, Tjellers happened to kill a lone impala, which almost walked right into the casually mobile group. Unfortunately for Tjellers and her offspring, a hyaena had been trailing us at some distance. Unbeknown to the mother leopard, killing the impala was the worst thing she could have done.

We did not even know the hyaena was there until he came charging in to the antelope's death cries. Immediately Tjellers realized her mistake and abandoned the carcass. But the two cubs were already so startled at having witnessed the aggression of their mother making 'their' first kill, that they froze in fear around the limp impala's body and failed to follow her up a tree to safety. In seconds the hyaena was there. Tjellers flew at it with all her vigour to keep it at bay. Luckily the hyaena was only intent upon stealing the kill, and had probably not seen the cubs, for if he had, no doubt he would have had little compunction in taking one of them instead.

Circling the kill the hyaena was trying to find the best point of access past the adult leopard's barrage of blows. She, on the other hand, was making quite sure she kept herself between the carcass and her two cubs. Round and round they went. Seconds felt like minutes and eventually the two cubs came to their senses and got the message to get the hell out of there! With the sound of Two and Four clawing their way up a large marula tree a few metres away, Tjellers too abandoned the kill once more to the persistent hyaena.

Leopards are opportunistic hunters, and will kill if presented with easy pickings, regardless of hunger or how sensible it may seem at the time. Two stories in particular are quite amusing. They were told to us by Douw Grobler who, at the time, was the Tshokwane ranger in the Kruger National Park. The one incident happened up near Letaba one year where hail had killed 27 impalas. Finding these unfortunate animals a short while after their mass demise, a leopard treed every one of them for an intended long-term feast. The other event took place down near Skukuza where

NILS KURE

OPPOSITE TOP *Despite their strength, agility and ferocious attitude leopards are unwilling to risk injury by defending a kill against marauding hyaenas and will usually give way.*
OPPOSITE BOTTOM *Cubs nervously watch the drama unfolding at the base of their refuge.*
ABOVE *Displaying all the stealth and poise that are the hallmarks of its kind, a leopard closes in on its prey.*

NILS KURE

NILS KURE

OPPOSITE AND ABOVE *Hunting becomes easier for leopards during the annual impala lambing season. The young antelope are easy to catch and cache, and with a carcass securely treed against theft, a female and her offspring can feed at their leisure.*

12 impalas had been captured and enclosed overnight in a *boma* (a traditional reed enclosure, originally designed to secure livestock from predation). Again a resourceful leopard took advantage of the situation. Finding his favourite food so conveniently trapped within this small enclosure and unable to escape, he killed and treed all 12 antelope. Ten of them were found the next morning in the same tree!

While leopards have no aversion to eating carrion, the two individuals mentioned above were in no way going to have enough time to consume all the food available to them before it became inedible. A lot of it would have had to go to waste.

Tjellers too, in the impala lambing season, would stockpile food if the pickings were good. There was one herd of impalas that frequented a small clearing just north of Rocky Crossing – within her territory – that she used to exploit quite regularly. In one evening during the first lambing season we were there, she killed three young lambs in quick succession, treeing each one before returning to the herd to take the next. Without first gutting the animals, she headed off to call her two cubs. On her return with Two and Four she took each cub to a tree and carcass of its own and then left them to their meals while moving off to feed on the third carcass herself. Once again our respect for her grew. Almost as if she knew she only needed three, she left the rest of the herd untouched for a later date. With her we never witnessed any wastage.

NILS KURE

CHRIS DAPHNE

ABOVE *The Hogvaal cub shows his arboreal prowess. Leopards are the only big African cats that are perfectly at home in the bushveld canopy.*
RIGHT *Tjellers and Stevie on the move. When little more than two months of age, cubs begin to accompany their mother on her territorial patrols and from kill to kill.*

JAMES RAWDON

A leopard cub with its kill – a large lizard.

The most we ever witnessed her kill in one evening was six animals. But some of these were smaller creatures: two impalas, two duikers, a quail and a korhaan. The two adult female impalas were stolen from her by hyaenas, as was the one duiker, while the two birds were eaten by her on the spot before moving on. The other duiker – her last kill – she secured up a tree where she and the cubs fed off it for a few days.

Tjellers hated to be foiled by her prey. Whenever she was seen by impala before she could make her final charge, they would snort the alarm, sometimes all grouping together as if to see her off. If she did move off they would follow her for quite some distance – it was almost as if the impalas felt safer keeping right behind her with the danger in full view, than by letting her disappear, where she might have an opportunity to circle them and try again. The expression on her face was easy to read: ears back, she would skulk off into the nearest undergrowth, not in the least bit impressed. Almost invariably a loud, echoing grunt would resound from the gully into which she had disappeared.

The strangest thing Tjellers killed during our stay had to be a four-metre-long rock python, although we can't be sure she actually killed it. Following her through an overgrown *donga*, we lost sight of her for a few minutes while seeking

PETER NICHOLSON

an accessible vehicle route through the gully. When we caught up with her on the other side, she was already carrying the snake to the base of a tree. What was most interesting about the event was the way in which she tried to feed off the carcass. Tjellers seemed to have great difficulty breaking into the snake's scaley hide. Most other carcasses drape comfortably and securely in the branches of the trees into which they are hoisted, the limbs of the animal helping to wedge it into position and preventing it from being reclaimed by gravity. A large python, however, has no convenient extremities to prevent it from sliding out of the tree.

Eventually, with her neck fast tiring under the strain of holding up such an uncooperative kill, Tjellers managed to wrap the reptile around one of the larger boughs with one of her paws. Still, with too much length on one side, the snake began to slip, and she lunged at the shorter end, clawing the body back into place. After many near drops she finally managed to balance out the weight and settle down to her next problem: trying to feed. Frustrated with the near impenetrable scales, and after only chewing a little on the head, she abandoned the carcass, leaving it looped around the boughs of the tree, and set off in search of something more 'considerate' to eat. Months later we witnessed her fighting with a much smaller python, which was successful in keeping her at bay.

ABOVE *Displaying an amusing lack of judgement a young male leopard stalks a two-ton white rhino. Needless to say the leopard was unsuccessful in its quest.*
OVERLEAF *A leopard with a scrub hare. Leopards have a wide-ranging diet and, depending on circumstances, will kill and eat almost anything to survive. Generally speaking, however, as they grow to adulthood they learn by experience to hunt those animals that provide the most benefit for the least effort or danger. Females will also catch but not kill smaller prey for their offspring, giving them the opportunity to practise their own hunting skills on the unfortunate victim.*

CHRIS DAPHNE

TABLE ONE	DEVELOPMENT PROGRESS OF TJELLERS' TWO CUBS (1993)
early January	born
8 March	start climbing trees
30 March	first show interest in a carcass (baby duiker)
12 April	first eat meat
18 June	first encounter with live with prey (while mother was still strangling it)
4 July	first drink water
7 July	last suckle
9 July	make their first kills (mice)
16 September	start marking over mother's scent markings
24 September	receive the only live animal from their mother (scrub hare)
6 October	a cub makes its first substantial kill (scrub hare)
12 December	a cub makes its first 'large' kill (baby impala)

TABLE TWO	TJELLERS' KILLS (MARCH 1993 TO MARCH 1995)	
impala	adult male	*21*
	adult female	*41*
	sub-adult male	*9*
	sub-adult female	*12*
	male 6–12 months old	*12*
	female 6–12 months old	*2*
	young 0–6 months old	*28*
	Total	**125**
duiker	male	*5*
	female	*16*
	Total	**21**
steenbok	male	*1*
	female	*6*
	Total	**7**
scrub hares		**53**
kudu (young)		**2**
Swainson's francolin		**1**
crested francolin		**2**
quail		**3**
korhaan (black-bellied and red-crested)		**2**
serval kittens		**2**
African wild cat		**1**
bushbuck		**1**
mice		**several**
python (not certain, may have been carrion)		**1**

PETER CHADWICK

GRAHAM MITCHELL-INNES

The only other incident we witnessed involving snakes was when one of the then eight-month-old cubs was struck in the eye by a small Mozambique spitting cobra. As could almost be expected it was super-inquisitive Four who got herself into trouble. Thankfully the strike was not accurate; although the eye was clearly irritated for many days after, we noticed no lasting effects other than a blackening of fur around the eye that stayed for a few months. Curiosity very nearly killed the cat!

It is largely believed by many that a leopard's favourite prey is the baboon. This is not the case. In fact, at Mala Mala, the leopards usually give these primates a wide berth. And quite justifiably too. Baboons are extremely aggressive when attacked. The whole troop will stand up to ward off any offensive, the noise alone usually proving sufficient deterrent to a potential predator. The large male baboons, of which there are usually a number in a single troop, have formidable sets of canines, and even a leopard would think twice before tangling with such opposition. In any event, there is such an abundance of easier prey around the Sand River, that there is no reason for a leopard to risk life and limb in finding its next meal. Possibly in areas where there is little else but baboon as a food source a leopard may well learn to specialize in hunting them. Presumably, even in such instances, the leopard would exercise great circumspection so as to minimize the chance of retaliation by the troop.

ABOVE *A leopard takes on an adult baboon. Although baboons are popularly thought to be a favourite prey of leopards, we find (certainly at Mala Mala) that the cats have a healthy respect for a baboon troop and almost never see the wily primates as potential food.*
OPPOSITE *Young leopards show an intense interest in anything that moves.*

CHRIS DAPHNE

Our leopards always had a great respect for the chacma baboons of the Lowveld. Vervet monkeys they would chase, yes, but never have I seen and only once have I heard of any leopard from Mala Mala showing an interest in a baboon as a meal. Having said that, however, on one occasion I did witness Tjellers charge down a lone adult male baboon over an open area. But the chase was not for food; it was rather just a show of aggression, even though it was without any provocation. At the start of the encounter she was a long way off and could not have felt immediately threatened by the baboon's presence. Furthermore, he was walking away from her and, as far as I could tell, had not even seen her before she charged him. Two and Four were at this time already semi-independent, so Tjellers' maternal, protective instincts could hardly have provided the motivation for the chase. She had not even been with them for a number of days. Yet for some reason she charged this baboon at a full run for over a hundred metres. The baboon himself seemed a little surprised, and, looking over his shoulder at her hasty approach he loped off towards the protection and escape provided by a *donga* and some trees.

Vervet monkeys sometimes present a more attractive target. We witnessed some of the younger leopards of Mala Mala avidly pursuing the agile vervet from tree to tree, displaying amazing success in many cases. It would appear, though, that it is only youthful cockiness that prompts a leopard to attack such alert, impossible-to-catch prey. Most adults will ignore the little primates screaming at them from a canopy of thin branches above.

The vervet is usually the bushveld's early warning system. Many pairs of eyes scanning the ground will notice the dappled cat walking in their direction from great distances. Tail twitching in irritation the adult leopard usually saunters on without so much as an upward glance. In our experience the whole troop could be going mad overhead and Tjellers wouldn't even so much as pause to give them a moment's notice.

Some leopards do try to catch monkeys, but not often with success. Nils Kure, now Mala Mala's manager, wrote what I think is a charming description of an encounter between monkeys and a young male leopard. 'The little monkeys were enraged; bobbing their heads up and down, bouncing around in the branches and approaching to within a few feet of their enemy to cough and grimace in his face, it seemed that their bodies were too frail to contain the passions within ... I found it very attractive to suppose that their pride as professional prey was outraged at the very idea that they might be caught by such a woeful incompetent ...'

Interestingly, though, when she was still a young leopard, Tjellers was just as interested in the feisty, furry grey creatures as any young cub of adolescent naiveté and, unlike the 'incompetent' described above, an adept hunter of them too. Many rangers witnessed her successes, and her skill was legendary. One troop in particular was chased so expertly and unceasingly that the individuals stopped trying to flee and clung trembling to the branches, unable to move. After terrorizing the troop to excess, she then caught one of its members with little effort, plucking it from the tree

NILS KURE

ABOVE *Impala, the most numerous of all the bushveld antelope species.*
OPPOSITE *A leopard with a vervet monkey. Monkeys often seem to taunt leopards with their raucous scolding, but generally they are too agile for leopards to catch and while young leopards are sometimes goaded into hunting vervets, most adults learn to ignore them.*

KIM WOLHUTER

ABOVE *A true creature of the dark – a lesser bushbaby. The chilling cry of these engaging mammals is one of the characteristic sounds of the bushveld night.*
OPPOSITE *Another case of a leopard's eyes being bigger than its stomach. The Hogvaal male was often found 'hunting' buffalo, but with no success. Here he suffers the indignity of being treed by a herd of the irascible grazers.*

like an overripe fruit and worrying it in mock attack, but inexplicably never killing it. Perhaps she was just honing her skills for later use. Today, in her latter years, she ignores them completely.

We were sometimes disappointed that we had not spent time with the Hogvaal female and cub, particularly when the maturing male began hunting alone as he approached adulthood. The Hogvaal *donga* is much closer to Mala Mala's Main Camp than the Tjellahanga River, and with most of the game-drive vehicles coming from up north, the majority of guest sightings were of the Hogvaal female and cub. With a dense network of roads throughout her territory they were the most regularly seen individuals on the property for those months. The terrain and bush up north is also somewhat easier to traverse and the temptation for the game drives to come down south to where we were was not too strong. The advantage of this was that we were pretty much left alone to get on with making our film without any outside distractions. Nonetheless, we were often frustrated by the reports about what the Hogvaal male cub was getting up to.

With the typical exuberance of youth, coupled with the added strength, size, weight and arrogance that usually characterizes male leopards, his opinion of his own hunting abilities was much inflated. Once he had grown past his mother's modest weight and size he seemed to think he was omnipotent. Almost weekly over the radio we would hear reports of his seemingly insane attempts at finding his daily bread: his eyes bigger than his stomach, he would stalk and hunt giraffe, adult kudu and wildebeest, and even a herd of buffalo. The outcome was predictable; he was totally out of his league and, to begin with, always came off second best. Yet he tried time and again for the same animals. Persistently he would stalk a herd of buffalo until one of them sensed his presence, and week after week he would find himself clambering up the nearest tree to safety. Sometimes even his selection of tree left much to be desired: small, spindly affairs, they only offered the scantiest of protection, just out of reach of the enraged buffalo bulls at its base.

One of his kills that did surprise and impress us all was a young zebra. A zebra foal alone is not beyond a male leopard's capabilities, but when one considers that the mother zebra and the other adults would have been in attendance at the kill and doing their utmost to defend the newest edition to the family group, one can only admire this leopard's gall. How he got away with it one cannot imagine.

His ultimate triumph, though, had to be the incident in which he attacked an adult kudu cow. Instead of taking the usual strategy of strangulation he jumped onto the cow's back in much the same manner as lions do when trying to subdue a buffalo. To take on an animal of this size and by adopting such a cautious approach the Hogvaal male presumably, for once, felt somewhat out of his depth, but went in for the challenge nonetheless. Like a cowboy trying to break in a stallion the leopard rode the cow for some time before it collapsed under his weight.

GRAHAM MITCHELL-INNES

CHRIS DAPHNE

CHAPTER THREE

Chauvinists

PETER CHADWICK

The leopard began to take up a lot of my thoughts.
And there was no man to whom
I could talk about it who would be able to help me
in any way. Even now, as I am telling you
this story, I am expecting you to wink at me, like
Krisyan Lemmer did. Still, I can only
tell you the things that happened as I saw them,
and what the rest was about only Africa knows.

Herman Charles Bosman
In the Withaak's Shade

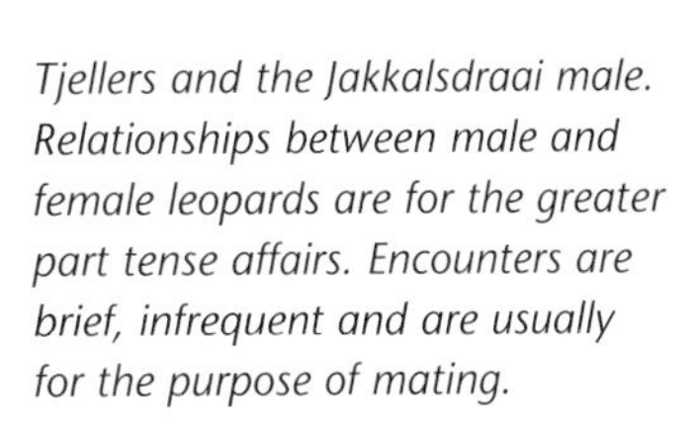

Tjellers and the Jakkalsdraai male. Relationships between male and female leopards are for the greater part tense affairs. Encounters are brief, infrequent and are usually for the purpose of mating.

PETER CHADWICK

The Jakkalsdraai male often tracked Tjellers down by following her scent.

Most leopard research to date has centred around females and their offspring. This is understandable as females are denser on the ground than their male counterparts and provide more 'material' to work with. Because they are more highly concentrated, females are easier to track, especially as their territories are smaller than those of males.

With their greater numbers and the added motivation of almost always having a litter of cubs to protect, females, in theory, also pose a greater potential for contacts with other females. In addition, the cubs are an obvious bonus in terms of research material. All in all, a far more productive situation than the supposed reclusive, ever meandering, solitary males. For the sake of our film we too decided on this logical approach. After all, we only had 17 months of shooting to make a 50-minute film on a cat with a legedary reputation of being able to elude man, even in and around the suburbs of some cities. Little did we know that with the regular surprise arrivals of the Jakkalsdraai male, all this was to change, and we would have to expand the film to an unprecedented 83 minutes in order to do justice to all that we were to see and record.

Two weeks into filming and we were already graced by his lordship's presence. It was predawn and we had been following Tjellers up one of the tributaries of the Tjellahanga riverbed towards the Kruger National Park; she was on her way back to her two cubs, now about two months of age. As previously recounted, at this early stage we were still having great difficulty trying to follow her. We didn't know the area well enough to get to and from various places with ease, and the dense summer vegetation seemed to block our every turn.

The cubs were still very young and Tjellers, not yet completely accustomed to being followed by our two vehicles, would choose very thick bush in which to hide them. It was dawn when we finally heard her and the two cubs calling to each other in greeting. Although only 20 or 30 metres away we could see little of them. This was as close as we were going to get for today. In another few weeks she would take them to a new hideaway, hopefully somewhere more accessible and open to viewing. But for now we were fighting the bush and our own frustrations. The cubs played for a while, and suckled, but it wasn't long before the rustling of the grass and occasional grunts from the cubs ceased, and all fell silent. They were asleep, and should have remained so throughout the heat of midday.

About to return to camp we heard a sharp, explosive puffing coming a little away from where we thought Tjellers and her cubs to be. Pausing, we again heard the unusual sound. Then we heard a similar sound from Tjellers – she was still in the thicket directly in front and seemed to be responding.

A short distance off we caught a very brief glimpse of a much larger leopard, evidently a male. Saliva drooling from his mouth, we found him very ugly compared to 'our' pretty females. And then he was gone, out of sight and into the thick bush where the female and her cubs were hidden. A few more puffs and all again fell silent. This was, to the best of our knowledge, the first time the cubs had met up with another leopard. Was this their father? Was he a vagrant, or the neighbouring, dominant male? In which case would he, as do lions, for example, try to kill the cubs fathered by another? The frustration and tension was terrible. We could do nothing. At first we just sat, ears straining, listening for anything that might give us a clue to what was happening beyond our view. At least nothing serious had taken place – yet.

We soon convinced ourselves that had the male posed a threat to the cubs' safety, their mother would surely have rushed out in defence of them on first hearing his approach. Or would she have? The male was much bigger than her modest 30 kilograms. Some males have tipped the scales at a massive 90 kilograms. Maybe his superior size and strength demanded unconditional submission born out of fear for her own safety – but this was unlikely. A female leopard's fierce reputation in the face of any danger did not point strongly in this direction. Everything indicated that she must have known this individual well. But even so, and as far as we knew, the cubs did not. If this was the first meeting between father and offspring, what would be the outcome? Would there be any tension? How close would their mother let him come? We tried to find other points of access to answer all our questions, but in vain.

Another explosive grunt emanated from the little social gathering as the male sawed a powerful communication to the others. We spotted the two little cubs scattering deeper into the undergrowth, clearly terrified by the volume and strength of his call. We were convinced we had just missed the only family gathering we were likely to see. Fortunately, we were wrong.

NILS KURE

Other than for the purpose of mating, male leopards are mostly attracted to females by the prospect of finding one of their caches.

Some weeks after this first encounter we were again sitting with Tjellers and her cubs, who were in a large marula tree not far from the Jakkalsdraai Open Area. It was the middle of the night; the kill was already a few hours old and the leopards were taking it in turns to feed. Tjellers had returned with the cubs some time earlier and potential for filming seemed to be long over. We were sitting silently in the dark, waiting for the moon to rise and listening to one of the cubs gnawing on the carcass. Suddenly a burst of hooves descended on us from behind. Slightly startled from our tranquil respite we both grabbed our spotlights and spun around to search for what was crashing towards us through the bush. Two or three impalas darted between our vehicles in the darkness during the time we took to react. Our lights clicking on simultaneously, we picked up the steady advance of the Jakkalsdraai male. Ever confident, his movements were decidedly deliberate and unhurried. In the days between these two encounters the rangers had verified that he was indeed the father of our two cubs.

Again a duet of 'prusten' commenced as both adult male and female sensed each other's presence. Prusten, or chuffling as it is more commonly known, is made by short, sharp bursts of exhaled air from the individual's mouth. Leopards are

QUINTON HADDON

As with domestic cats, leopards are fanatical about grooming and keeping clean.

thought to make the sound as a form of greeting and reassurance; a sort of 'Hello, it's me; I come in peace.' In the months that followed, however, we did witness some circumstances where it also seemed to denote a certain amount of tension and insecurity on the part of one of the individuals, almost as if the one leopard was asking for reassurance as to the other's motives. For the moment though, this was our first male/female rendezvous out in the open where we were able to observe clearly, and to film, what took place.

Nothing seemed out of place and, after a brief nose-to-nose greeting between the two adults, the male ascended the tree and commandeered the kill; his unchallenged right as a male. Not that the cubs seemed to mind at this age, mind you. Whilst receiving most of their nourishment from mother's milk, feeding on meat

NILS KURE

The Mlowathi male in repose. Even at rest, the latent energy and aggression of a male leopard is evident.

was still more of a game and a learning experience for them than the serious business of survival it would become with time. For now they seemed far more interested in biting dad's tail and flanks while he gorged himself on his new-found bounty.

The Jakkalsdraai male's territory not only overlapped that of Tjellers, but those of a number of her neighbours as well. It soon emerged that the attraction was twofold: Firstly he would check on the sexual receptivity of the female and then he would look around for any food, but almost certainly would not show any distinctly paternal instincts or social needs. Whenever he picked up the fresh scent of the adult female, he would follow it relentlessly until he had tracked her down. Usually this would lead him back to one of her kills. By moving off to fetch her cubs and returning to her kills, she would unintentionally leave a bold advertisement of her presence in the area for

DALE HANCOCK

Tjellers hoists her kill up a tree. The Mala Mala leopards' most common prey is the impala – in this case a young sub-adult male.

him to follow. Any available food would then be expropriated by him, both mother and cubs stepping down from the kill to wait their turn.

In such circumstances, his superiority was not to be questioned by anybody and would be reinforced by some stiff blows if need be. In his defence though, he did show admirable tolerance of the cubs. Although in appearance quite harsh, his disciplining of them was never excessive or injurious. There was simply no need to 'speak' twice. Were it not for the free meal on offer, however, we doubt he would ever have bothered to track them down and suffer their company. But once food was included in the deal, the life of matrimony and fatherhood seemed much to his satisfaction.

Sometimes it seemed to us that Tjellers had invented a strategy for outwitting the Jakkalsdraai male and his scrounging habits. For the first year of the cubs' lives, she would go off periodically, patrolling her territory until she managed to make a kill. Shortly after treeing the carcass, usually without feeding, she would promptly set off to fetch her cubs. On finding them and once the ritual greetings had taken place, they would return directly to the carcass. On arrival Tjellers would always let the cubs feed first.

These return trips to the kill were usually over the shortest possible distance; rivers, koppies (small hills), and the like considered. It was on one of these trips with the two cubs in tow that the Jakkalsdraai male happened upon this now familiar trio. Knowing what a good provider she was, he happily tagged along. No doubt within a few seconds his saliva would have begun flowing in antici-pation of the coming banquet. Once again it appeared he would end up the benefactor of Tjellers' hard work. Much to our pleasure though, it soon became evident that Tjellers was one step ahead of the situation. Within a few hundred metres she veered off on a totally new bearing. This change of course took place early in the evening, and by daybreak the next morning, after a very long and taxing night, we had covered the full extremities of her territory, and then some.

Needless to say, when he finally tired of the futile marathon, a much leaner male went off to look for a meal of his own. It seemed his patience was not as great as his hunger. Tjellers promptly led the now exhausted cubs to her kill only a short distance away. We found much humour in the situation, and to our minds, so did she.

Irrational as it might have been, we were highly irritated by just how often the Jakkalsdraai male stole kills from Tjellers and the cubs, and presumably the other females in his territory. But he did occasionally kill for himself as well.

We noticed a few minor differences between the way the Jakkalsdraai male and Tjellers behaved with reference to their stashes. Over time we were able to confirm these by drawing parallels with other male and female leopards on the property. The males seemed to dedicate far more time to 'plucking' their victims before feeding than did the females. Quite often the females would not even bother, whereas the males would spend ages plucking an impala of its hair before opening it up to feed. Strangely, the male leopard would spend all this

CHRIS DAPHNE

Tjellers was always happiest when alone and not being followed by her male shadow, the Jakkalsdraai male.

time cleaning the animal's side and stomach, and then open up the carcass through the anus. The anus is always the most convenient and easiest place to feed from. It is the softest point of access. Yet why then spend all that wasted time plucking the fur from the flank, which from that point on is ignored? The leopard clearly does not enjoy the task: with wrinkled nose and upper lip raised as far out of the way as possible, the leopard spits and shakes his head to try and rid himself of the fine hairs that stick to his teeth and tongue.

The males would also often leave their carcasses for many hours on end and go 'walkabout' before returning, much later, to feed again. They seemed to have a constant need to travel. Maybe the size of their territories demanded this of them in order to maintain a regular enough presence on all their boundaries

QUINTON HADDON

Leopards get most of their liquid needs from the prey they consume, but they enjoy fresh water where it is available.

where other dominant males might be looking for an extra few acres of turf. The females seemed far more content to spend all their time lounging about in the boughs of a nearby tree, with their kill in clear view. Obviously, if caring for young cubs the females would have to leave their carcasses to either suckle or fetch the cubs, but once relieved of this responsibility, we never once saw the females leave their kills until they were completely finished feeding.

The most interesting and unexpected interaction we witnessed between individual leopards occurred one evening with the Tjellahanga female and the Jakkalsdraai male. On this occasion a small pride of lionesses had been trailing Tjellers for some time. Later, after losing them and being very much on edge, her mate arrived on the scene. Usually the leopards would come together, sniff each other, both chuffling profusely, and move off in tandem. The Jakkalsdraai male too, would usually announce his arrival by calling a few times as he neared, hoping for a reply. On this occasion, however, probably sensing the close proximity of the lions, he chose to sneak up on her. By now, very much on edge and in no mood for surprises, she kept avoiding him, eventually taking refuge in a tree, yeowling at his advances.

We had never seen her react in this way, and were intrigued as to what would happen next. Very careful not to disturb her and stalking to within metres of where she lay unawares in the lower branches of the tree, he pounced into the long grass below only to sit back and watch her reaction. Totally surprised, and much to his apparent pleasure, she clambered up into the higher reaches of the tree. It seemed to us an act of sheer bedevilment on his behalf.

Even after some time had passed Tjellers steadfastly refused to greet him. Not to be denied and now at the end of his tether, the Jakkalsdraai male followed her into the upper reaches of the tree and gave her a hiding incomparable to anything we had seen. The beating left her swinging by only one paw from the branch below him and, apparently now satisfied that she had been appropriately chastised, he continued on his way, leaving her to lick her wounds.

With such strained relations between male and female, mating in leopards is understandably a tense affair. In a behaviour pattern similar to lions, a female leopard will entice a male by running back and forth in front of him, from left to right, and then by lying down with her tail almost wrapped around his face in anticipation and expectation. If he is interested he will mount; if not she will soon spring up and continue with her flirtations. In the early stages it is a confusion of desire and tension where every time the male approaches, the female will turn on him and chase him off. By the look on his face at this point the male does not appreciate the teasing, but tries to keep his cool and maintain

QUINTON HADDON

One of the most impressive events one can hope to witness must be leopards mating. The sound and aggression is incredible.

a certain amount of self-pride, as if the situation is all under control. In the end he will get what he wants.

When mating commences, the two are committed to days of strolling around the male's territory, seldom breaking from their routine even to hunt. Because leopards are opportunistic hunters by nature, they did make some kills that were too easy to pass up, but the pair seemed to show little interest in feeding and would generally abandon the food before it was finished and resume their meanderings.

After coming into oestrus again some 10 months after giving birth to her two cubs, Tjellers and the Jakkalsdraai male again mated. On the fourth day of their intercourse they came across Two and Four. Usually a mother leopard would abandon her cubs to their own devices for the full duration of her mating, so bumping into them was unexpected and presumably unintentional. It was not long before the cubs witnessed their mother thrashing around in front of their father and the ensuing mating. The two youngsters were not impressed by the animated display and the vocal volume of their parents' efforts and fled for cover into the undergrowth.

Initially we were very excited at the prospect of having Tjellers give birth to another litter of cubs. Now that she was so used to our presence this would provide us with the opportunity of filming day-old cubs, something we had not been able to achieve with Two and Four. Not only this, but by the time these new cubs were due to be born, both Two and Four would still be relatively dependent on their mother and she would either be forced to care for two litters simultaneously or to chase the older two away somewhat prematurely, with the possibility of some interesting interactions.

A double litter would have constituted a real 'rosette of leopards'! We had heard of one such incident from East Africa, where as many as six leopards were

PIETER DROS

Mating seems to be a strange paradox of attraction and antagonism.

NILS KURE

ABOVE *The Hogvaal female and her cub. The bond between mother and cub lasts well into the second year of a cub's life.*
OPPOSITE *A male patrols his vast territory.*

seen together in the same tree: and with the adult male in attendance they would have numbered seven.

But this was not to be: a month later Tjellers was found mating again. Conception had obviously not taken place. And a month after that she was mating yet again. Her monthly mating sessions went on for some eight months, and we started to wonder if there was something wrong with her. With three to six days of mating, at a frequency similar to that of lions, how could she not conceive? Now, at eight years of age, she was in prime reproductive condition.

In total Tjellers and the Jakkalsdraai male had eight separate mating sessions, over as many months. But on one occasion, whilst on the fourth day of intercourse, she heard a male calling off to the northwest. Almost immediately she headed that way. Females usually follow the males around while mating, but this time roles were reversed. The Jakkalsdraai male, aware of what was happening, kept trying to cut her off. Try as he may, though, he did not succeed. As we already had plenty of footage of leopards mating on previous occasions, we had been tempted to leave and go searching for something else to film. With this rather unexpected turn of events, however, we were compelled to follow. Every time the male leopard tried to cut her off Tjellers would crouch down, hissing her disapproval. Eventually, quite a distance beyond the boundary of her territory and on the outer extremities of his, they met up with the newcomer; the Mlowathi male.

The Mlowathi male was a favourite amongst the rangers. He had grown up close to Main Camp and had by this stage commandeered the northernmost farms, which are frequented by most of the game-drive traffic. He had become an exceptionally relaxed individual. Perhaps because he was usually seen at close quarters, he gave the impression of being much bigger than any other male, an observation touted by the rangers when they told of him sniffing at their shoes through the open driver's door of their Land Rover.

To the best of our knowledge Tjellers' and the Mlowathi male's territories were not adjoining, and yet she had purposefully sought him out. Was she also aware of and concerned about her inability to conceive? Was this in some way an attempt by her to fall pregnant by means of another male? Although Tjellers showed all the appropriate submissiveness to the new male, he seemed unimpressed. More than unimpressed, in fact, for he reacted violently to this highly attractive and available female smothered with the scent of one of his greater sexual opponents, and gave her a good hiding.

The relationship between Tjellers and the Mlowathi male soon settled, however, and the Jakkalsdraai male was chased back to his home territory by his rival, with much calling between the two. Tjellers then wandered off with her new consort right into the heart of his territory. She was now a long way from home, with the territories of a number of other females in-between. After her mating interlude, under the protection of her new suitor, she would be left to negotiate her own way home unescorted, through the territories held by competing females. It appears that the majority of female meetings take place whilst trespassing in another's territory under the protection of a mating male partner.

Tjellers' attempt to fall pregnant by the Mlowathi male, if that is what it was, was also unsuccessful as she was seen a month later, again mating with the Jakkalsdraai male. But then, much to our delight, in January of 1995, just one month before we were due to leave Mala Mala, she gave birth to a single cub. Our filming was coming to an end and so we would have just a few all-too-short weeks to film her latest addition to the continuing Tjellahanga line. We were lucky; not only did we get some really useful shots of the cub in its lair over this period, but on the last day of filming for *Beauty and the Beasts*, Tjellers carried her two-week-old cub in broad daylight to a new, safer venue, away from the prowling attentions of hyaenas.

Later, from research on leopard behaviour, we learnt that leopard mating sessions are usually only 15 per cent successful, with conception only taking place sometimes after as many as eight such mating interludes. Perhaps then, what we had perceived as Tjellers' difficulty in falling pregnant, is, in fact, quite normal?

NILS KURE

DALE HANCOCK

A male black-bellied korhaan. This species is a common resident of the Lowveld where its favoured habitat is the rank vegetation of moist grasslands.

But is the biology of the animal and its likelihood to conceive in any way influenced by the seasons? Seven litters of cubs were born to the leopards in the area during our filming. These were all between September and February. No births occured in the winter months. Maybe it is quite normal for most matings to fail if mating takes place in the wrong season. Could the Tjellahanga female have fallen pregnant during one of those earlier matings and then simply miscarried?

One way or the other, none of that mattered now. Delayed or not, we had a new cub to watch and enjoy. Fortunately, another new project on leopards, following directly after *Beauty and the Beasts*, allowed me a few more months of work with Tjellers and her new cub. Looking back, we could never be certain that what we had witnessed many months before had been the first meeting between the Jakkalsdraai male and the two cubs. After our initial excitement during the meeting (from what we could see and hear of it), the eventual outcome was a bit of an anticlimax. Maybe the two leopards had met before under much tenser circumstances and were already old acquaintances. This time round with the new cub, I could see for certain what a first encounter between father and cub was like.

Predictably, within two weeks of the cub's birth, the Jakkalsdraai male found Tjellers and her cub at the new lair. It was early in the morning, shortly after she had returned to suckle her wobbly bundle of fur amongst the rocks. The game-drive vehicles were following the male, so I knew he was nearby and was following the female's route into the lair – the same one she had led me on just before dawn. He lost her scent for a while only a few hundred metres up the *donga*. He milled around and doubled back on himself to make sure exactly which way she had gone before proceeding in my direction.

Tjellers saw him but showed no response. Lying on her side, with the cub still suckling, she watched with the unblinking stare so characteristic of a leopard as he padded his way down the sand towards them. She was the first to start the puffs of prusten and, picking up on the sound, the male trotted in. The cub stopped suckling and rolled more than walked towards the Jakkalsdraai male. He pushed his way under the thick bush that served as partial protection from any potential danger. Still Tjellers lay there, unperturbed. Almost all previous greetings between her and the male had been electric, with Tjellers showing distinctly nervous submission. Yet in this situation she was totally at peace. Father and cub sniffed each other over for a while and soon the male lay down, and allowed the cub to bite and pull at his ears. The trust Tjellers showed in the Jakkalsdraai male was impressive. I would never have expected it.

The name we settled on for this new cub was 'Stevie'. The rangers expected us to choose another number, but we were not about to be that predictable. The name was derived from our initial decision of 'Evens-Stevens' or '3–3 Steve', which as one might guess is because he had three whisker spots on either side of his face. We could not say what sex the cub was, but we guessed it was male, simply because Tjellers' previous cubs were both females. Only some months after we had left did we receive news from our friends the rangers that the he was in fact a she. We were tempted to rename the cub 'Stephanie', but Stevie she remained. Today, as a mature territorial animal, she has been named 'the Harry's female' in accordance with Mala Mala's practice.

An interesting piece of information regarding one of Tjellers' cubs (Two) came from a game-drive sighting of her, also some months after we had completed filming on the project. She was found mating, at the age of about 26 months, with her confirmed father, the Jakkalsdraai male. Not only was this quite early for her to be mating, but she had not yet been forced away from her mother's territory and into the dense population of other females in the area.

This all seems against the norms of behaviour involving a parent's tolerance towards its offspring after adulthood. Yet shortly after this, in the north of the Mala Mala property, the Hogvaal female and her male cub were also reported to have been seen mating. His father, the Mlowathi male, had disappeared some months earlier and the cub had, therefore, stayed on in his parents' territories. Females do not chase their male cubs out of their territory. This is left to the father to deal with, but in this instance the father was not around and he was now presumably dead. What did this mean genetically? To our knowledge neither of these two parent/offspring matings was successful.

Perhaps this was not surprising. After all, we knew that Tjellers mated over eight separate sessions before conceiving her latest cub.

DALE HANCOCK

ABOVE AND BELOW *Stevie meets her father. They sniffed each other over for a while and soon the male lay down. He allowed the cub to bite and pull at his ear.*

Male leopards have territories that are much bigger than those of females, and the Jakkalsdraai and Mlowathi males defended most of the six farms making up the Mala Mala property. But there was still a third, equally relaxed individual known to make brief appearances in a corner of the southernmost farm. This was the Flockfield male, or 'Flockies', as he was known to us. Almost as regular as clockwork, this 'old man' would parade past Harry's Camp along the eastern or western banks of the Sand River.

As relaxed as either of the other two, Flockies was for us the smartest male on the property and sported an interesting history. We liked to refer to him as 'the teddy bear' for although only as old as Tjellers, his skin hung loosely from his sizeable body, especially about the head and neck. When walking, his large dewlap swung back and forth, and his progress was always slow and confident. Walking or resting, his mouth was invariably open, giving his face a rounded, most endearing, chubby look, like a big, animated teddy bear, with a striking resemblance to a tiger. Even his temperament seemed to fit his appearance.

NILS KURE

Our first real encounter with Flockies was when we came across him fighting hyaenas over a kill. This is mainly what caused us to hold him in such high esteem. He was the only leopard we had witnessed who would engage in full contact, and was capable of sending an adult hyaena packing, much to our delight! On more

NILS KURE

ABOVE *The Mlowathi male. Males have distinctly thick, muscular necks and shoulders and most, in time, develop loosely hanging dewlaps.*

than one occasion, after charging in to the death cries of some animal, a hyaena would be seen scurrying off, backside to the ground with its back legs trying to overtake its head.

In his youth Flockies was also known to be a proficient hunter of large, adult male warthogs, and we hoped he would provide us with such a spectacle for our film. In Gerald Hind's book, *Leopard*, which also concentrates on the leopards of Mala Mala, the prowess of Flockies (called Nduna in Hind's work) as a warthog specialist is a strong feature. Although published some years prior, Gerald Hind's book was a constant source of hope to us film makers. Unfortunately for us, though, Flockies' more recent years seemed to find him abandoning such brave attempts for easier, less dangerous prey.

CHRIS DAPHNE

We liked to think of Flockies as 'lord of the manor', but the reality of the situation was that he was losing his authority, and fast. His name clearly indicated where his original stronghold had been, much further north, on the farm Flockfield, at this point the mutual boundary held by the Jakkalsdraai and Mlowathi males. Much care is taken not to name any Mala Mala leopard prematurely as, in the case of a newly independent sub-adult, the individual will drift for quite a time between dominant individuals' territories before settling in a vacant or fringe area that it is confident it is capable of defending. In the case of female leopards, once they have established a territory, they seldom drift much from this chosen area, living in it until their death. Males, on the other hand, are somewhat different. With their much larger territories, their annual movements seem to be in a state of constant flux.

ABOVE *Tjellers and Two, now almost fully grown.*
OVERLEAF *For the first 10 months of a cub's life both mother and cub will patrol and share the adult's territory.*
PHOTOGRAPH: CHRIS DAPHNE

PIETER DROS

Leopards don't like getting wet. Sometimes in summer the Sand River rises quickly, trapping individuals for a time on the wrong side. Here the Jakkalsdraai male bounds through the water.

Territorial fights do occur. In 1992 all the staff and guests of Mala Mala Main Camp were treated to the sight of a full-scale fight between two males just below the lunch deck. Standing up tall on their hind legs, the competitors apparently slashed out and tussled with one another like two bears. Such all out contests are rare, however, as not only is the outcome usually serious and potentially fatal for one or both parties, but more often than not, one of the males will usually be intimidated enough to back off long before such a skirmish becomes necessary. Far more usually the battles for territory are a matter of gradual wearing down. Our experiences of Flockies and the Jackalsdraai male provided a classic example.

By the time we came to know him, Flockies' territory had clearly changed quite drastically and the core of his turf had moved an estimated 40 kilometres to the southeast of where he had started out as an adult. Both the Jakkalsdraai and, in turn, Mlowathi males were now making clear demands on more and more land to the south.

NILS KURE

The incomparable Flockfield male. By now he was nearing the end of his prime and was being systematically ousted from his territory by the Jakkalsdraai male.

For a period in 1994 the Jakkalsdraai and Flockfield males used to meet daily for nearly two weeks running at a certain, invisible boundary line between their respective territories. Parading shoulder to shoulder, up and down on the western bank of Boomer's Crossing, the two would try to intimidate each other into backing down. To begin with neither was prepared to give in, and we were doubtful of the Jakkalsdraai male's superiority. If one got ahead of the other, it would try to move across the laggard's path, but in response the rival would run to cut it off. If either stopped they would both scrape mark, roll on their backs and rub their heads on the ground. The conflict strangely never went further than this impressive, very intimidating show of force.

Eventually, Flockies conceded defeat and gave another small chunk of his land over to the Jakkalsdraai male. From that day on we never saw Flockies as far north again. On future border patrols, at the more typical three- to four-day intervals, he would veer off east for the Kruger National Park, some distance shy

of the spot where the daily show-down had taken place. By the time we left, only about a tenth of his time was spent on the Mala Mala property. He began to occupy the large plot of dense, uncharted bushveld to the east of the reserve, inside the Kruger National Park. For the game-viewing vehicles, it became a race against time to catch up with him before he crossed over to the other side of the boundary and the rangers finally decided the small chance of reward did not warrant the time and effort spent in trying to track him down.

At the time of writing, Flockies is 14 years old and still out there. But, he is ageing, and will, in time, become one of the legends of the past, making up just one of the 'spots' in the ever-increasing rosette of Mala Mala leopards.

RICHARD DU TOIT

ABOVE *Giraffe drinking. These tall mammals are at their most vulnerable from attack by lions when satisfying their thirst.*
OPPOSITE *Leopards salivate when confronted by another of their sex. This must surely be the height of stress a leopard can experience.*

PHOTOGRAPH: NILS KURE

TABLE THREE	*MALE INTERACTION WITH TJELLERS FEMALE AND CUBS*
number of times males interacted with female and cubs	28
• interaction involving a carcass	17
• interaction with no carcass involved	11
male hung around feeding and left only when carcass was finished	5
male hung around to benefit from female's hunting or for social reasons	8
male arrived at carcass already well fed	1
male calls before arriving at the family	12
male feeds and leaves	
• after finishing the carcass	6
• without finishing the carcass	2
number of times the male's presence was in any way beneficial to the family	4

TABLE FOUR	*MALE LEOPARD INTERACTIONS*
number of times males interacted	12
interactions involving parallel marches	6
interactions where one male chased off the other through intimidation	2
interactions over a kill	1
both males calling to each other but without interactivity	2
interactions when mating	1

KIM WOLHUTER & DALE HANCOCK

CHAPTER FOUR

Confrontation

DALE HANCOCK

During this considerable period much no doubt has been learned, but also much has had to be unlearned. It is so easy to misunderstand the factors governing the actions and reactions of wild creatures living under natural conditions.

Colonel James Stevenson-Hamilton
Wild Life in South Africa

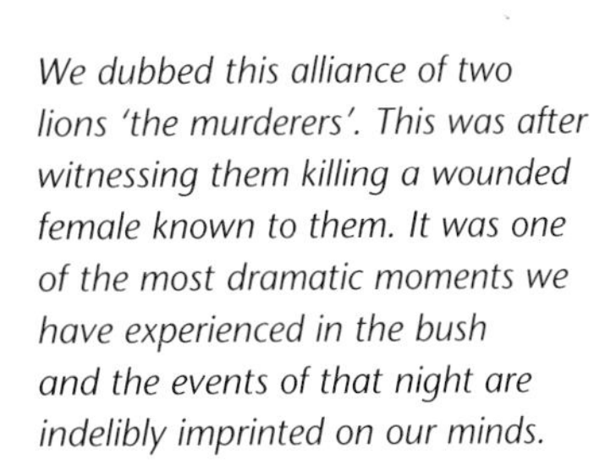

We dubbed this alliance of two lions 'the murderers'. This was after witnessing them killing a wounded female known to them. It was one of the most dramatic moments we have experienced in the bush and the events of that night are indelibly imprinted on our minds.

A portrait of Four, now rapidly growing up. Two was always the more cautious of the pair, and while Four was always ready to engage us, Two would hold back, obviously curious but lacking the extravert boldness of her sibling.

Although undocumented in the film *Beauty and the Beasts*, fighting between leopards is by no means uncommon, both between adults of the same sex, adults of differing sex, and the more common case of mother and soon-to-become-independent offspring.

Once they reach 20 months of age, female leopard cubs will gradually, over the coming weeks and months, be chased away by their mothers. This usually starts as a hiss from the adult whenever the cub approaches for its customary head butt and rub. The rebuff bares a faint resemblance to a snap from a dog when protecting a tasty morsel from a fellow sibling: nothing too serious, but making it quite clear the intruder is not welcome; although in the case of the leopard done with somewhat more style and control. At first the cub doesn't seem to know what to make of the rebuff and appears quite startled and puzzled. After much patience, and some weeks later, if the cub still resists the subtle messages to move on, the mother eventually resorts to force to prompt it on its way. Male cubs, on the other hand, will be allowed to stay on by their mothers, although they usually end up being chased off by the resident male who, in most instances is their father.

These parent-offspring encounters, particularly between a mother and her female cubs, can be savage and two that we witnessed only ended when the vanquished party fell from the tree that had served as the battleground. Even though still somewhat smaller than their parent, the cubs put up not only an amazing defence, but a formidable attack as well. In both fights we saw, the adult by no means commanded the higher odds, which demonstrates how the motivation to engage in physical violence has to be strong enough to outweigh the disadvantages of possible injury that might be fatal to the individual in the long run.

Reproducing adult female leopards, with the safety and protection of their cubs to consider, are also far more likely to be provoked into serious conflict with their neighbours than are their male counterparts. In the interests of their cubs rather than themselves, these female battles too are usually far more vicious than anything one might generally expect from male encounters.

In the few weeks prior to the birth of Stevie, Tjellers became very intent on demarcating her territory against intruders, even to the extent of crossing a good distance south of the Sand River to do so; something she seldom did at any other time, before or after. She seemed to be set on pushing the extremities of her boundaries just that little bit further than usual. The further away she could keep the neighbouring females, the less chance there would be of them trespassing and finding her cub at the lair, situated towards the centre of her territory.

The western boundary presented her with a problem, however. This was the home of the Trollips Crossing female, who was thought to be Tjellers' sister, but now (as adults) her rival and enemy. Trollips, as she was known, had also given birth to two cubs a number of months after the appearance of Two and Four, and at this stage these two younger cubs, although still essentially reliant on their mother, were beginning to make tentative steps towards finding territories of their own. This meant pushing out beyond the safety of their mother's home and, from time to time, trespassing on Tjellers' turf. Tjellers, in her heightened state of alertness to such activities, was very quick to pick up on the trespassing mother and cubs and to respond to this. With the evident build-up of traffic on her western boundary, Tjellers started making more and more frequent turns in this neck of the woods to see off intruders and to prevent the competition from gaining a foothold on her hard-won block of real estate.

Leaving Charleston Koppies, the large rocky outcrop she had chosen as the lair for the newborn Stevie, now only days old, Tjellers headed down towards Ingwe Donga, the recognized boundary between her and Trollips' territories. During the five days following Stevie's birth Tjellers had been almost entirely holed up within the lair, and it was time for her to reaffirm her boundaries. As usual she was marking regularly all the way, resting up a couple of times, but never longer than five minutes. She still could not afford too much time away from her tiny cub. Then, at a point in the *donga* where a long ridge of rocks runs down into the riverbed itself (an area we called Running Rocks), she picked up the scent of Trollips and her two cubs. The rangers had seen all three of them together in this area over these past few days.

The change in Tjellers was immediate. This scent was far too fresh! And there were three intruders, all essentially adults. To make matters worse, only a short distance off was Mister's Koppies, another of the preferred lair sites she would rotate between after Charleston Koppies and a few other select sites had been used. In fact Mister's Koppies was historically always her second choice, and the only remaining good, rocky outcrop available after Charleston Koppies, even though it was situated dangerously close to Ingwe Donga. (*Ingwe* means leopard in the local Shangaan dialect.)

Sniffing around intently Tjellers would roll on her back at certain spots where the scent was most tantalizing, presumably where Trollips and cubs had all lain down a few metres apart. Following the scent of the trio she headed off down the *donga* at a steady pace. She gave a fast yet quiet grunt, which she cut short half way through, as if expecting to hear the panicked scatterings of three intimidated cats disappearing into the nearby thicket. She paused to listen. No such luck.

The scent now getting stronger, she began to trot. The intruders had to be close by. The pace was heavy going and leaving the *donga* she crossed south over Jock Walk. With Kim battling to keep up with her, she ran down into the next *donga*. There was a brief commotion as she surprised and flushed Trollips. Caterwaulling as she went, Trollips was chased for about 150 metres before Tjellers caught her. The contact was brief and vicious. Then they split, standing face to face only two metres apart, growling with hatred and antagonism. They had inflicted almost identical, gaping wounds on each other during the explosive scrap – a perfect match.

JAMES RAWDON

Tjellers and Stevie in the comparatively safe surroundings of their rocky lair.

NILS KURE

Scraping at the ground with their hind legs is one of the ways in which leopards mark their territories, a warning signal to a rival leopard that it is trespassing.

DALE HANCOCK

For the most part we found Tjellers to be an even-tempered animal. Certainly she was very tolerant of us. But when the occasion would demand it, as in the instance of her encounter with the Trollips Crossing female, she was all aggression.

Neither leopard seemed keen on initiating another contact and, in the manner more typical of a male show-down, they headed off back north, side by side and parallel to Ingwe Donga. As they were just west of the *donga* it seemed as if Tjellers was holding the psychological advantage. Both scrape marked and rolled as they went, with Trollips calling for her two cubs, although neither was brave enough to come out in support, if that was what she had intended. Shoulder to shoulder and salivating, Tjellers and Trollips patrolled northwards until they lay down some five metres apart to rest.

After about 10 minutes, Tjellers rose and gave a mock charge in her opponent's direction, but raised no response from her whatsoever. Seemingly having saved a little face from her nonchalance, Trollips, after a further 20 minutes of ignoring Tjellers' protestations, rose and headed off back from where she had come, scraping as she went. Waiting to be sure she was safely out of the way, Tjellers then went and rolled where her adversary had marked, and followed up one last time to confirm that Trollips had definitely left the area.

Dale Hancock

A lioness watches intently through recently burnt bush – a leopard is nearby. The lions will not tolerate its presence and will pursue it. A leopard has no chance against the numbers and bulk of a lion pride and will always try to make good its escape in any confrontation.

Some weeks after the birth of Stevie, a now practically independent Two also happened to stumble across Tjellers and Stevie lying at the lair. Two had presumably tracked her mother down as she so often had in the past, in the hope of being accepted around her mother's table. Strangely, even after the process of attempting to chase her cubs away was well in progress, Tjellers still occasionally allowed the now essentially independent Two and Four to feed off her kills, but only if the twosome managed to find her of their own accord and as a result of their own resourcefulness.

This time, however, as one could well expect, Tjellers lost no time in sending Two packing. Long before Two could even get within reasonable distance of the lair, Tjellers flew from the rocks and chased her offspring for over two kilometres at a full run, game-drive vehicles bumping along behind, until the 'intruder' was on the edge of her mother's territory. Only here did Tjellers slow and then stop to scrape the ground with her hind legs in a demonstration of her rightful possession of her territory.

PETER I. CHADWICK

PETER I. CHADWICK

Large predators such as lions and hyaenas pose the greatest threat to leopards. We witnessed hyaenas stealing impala kills before the leopard could tree them almost as a weekly event. Not long after we started following Tjellers on her nightly escapades, hyaenas would come to investigate the telltale droning of our two vehicles, joining in the procession as we followed the meanderings of our subject. These supreme opportunists were very quick to pick up on the fact that if they hung around for long enough, the leopard would catch something. They, as the more powerful individuals, would then be able to take the meal from her. It is common knowledge that leopards tree their kills for exactly this reason. We found that in the north of the property, where the hyaena numbers were substantially lower than down south, the leopards seldom hoisted their kills into trees, finding it easier to feed off them on the ground.

Initially Tjellers' kills varied widely in weight and size. She was not in the least averse to bringing down large prey. If something reasonable came within reach, she went for it. Many of her kills were adult impala, males included. If left unmolested by rival predators, leopards will just as soon feed on the ground, thereby avoiding exerting themselves by hoisting a meal heavier than themselves to the safety of a tree. But then the visits from her enemies, the hyaenas, became disconcertingly frequent. The effort of treeing large kills became too exacting. With the scavengers hot on her heels and her chest still heaving from the chase, not to mention the victim still kicking and knocking her off balance, it was not surprising that Tjellers would lose the majority of these prizes. She therefore became more selective, taking only smaller animals that she could whip up a tree to safety, in the process foiling the hyaenas charging in bellow.

Hyaenas are regarded as being amongst the most intelligent inhabitants of the African bush, although a number of encounters gave us reason to doubt their status. Leopards kill their larger prey by strangulation and sometimes this is a relatively drawn out process. For example, adult impalas caught by a leopard often manage to remain on their feet for some time before collapsing from suffocation. Even after falling, it can still take a while before they finally succumb. On one particular occasion, just as Tjellers' victim had collapsed, a young hyaena homed in on the commotion. His vision of what was going on was obscured by long grass and our vehicles, but, excited by a sound he knew only too well, he ran in at full tilt to steal the kill. The hyaena's clumsy approach gave Tjellers ample time to react and, as usual, she chose discretion as the best strategy. Knowing it futile to try to protect her prize, she abandoned it in the interests of her own safety.

The frightened impala was far from beaten, however, and once released, jumped up and bolted. Hyaenas are excitable creatures at the best of times and this one, as with most inexperienced youngsters, was so wound up that he blindly chased the leopard instead of the now mobile impala. At least one thief went hungry that evening. This was cause for great celebration on our part and we promptly broke for a coffee break.

NILS KURE

OPPOSITE AND ABOVE
A typical nightly scenario between leopard and hyaena. The leopard makes a kill, but before she has a chance to eat the impala on the spot, or carry it up a tree to safety, the hyaenas, which have probably been following the leopard, move in. The leopard swings round at the hyaena's approach, but she cannot risk injury and so, after a token attempt to defend her meal, she has to give in and take refuge up a tree.

Tjellers soon took to catching only smaller impala. By means of this strategy she was able to subdue her prey and hoist it up a tree in double-quick time, thereby foiling the hyaena pack that was more often than not hard on her heels.

When it came to hunting, Tjellers was quite simply fearless. On the odd occasion she even showed interest in giraffe, although I doubt with much serious intent. Possibly one of the most impressive kills we saw Tjellers make (like with the Hogvaal male) was a kudu that she even managed to tree. Although not fully grown, the kudu was still heavier than any impala we had seen her hoist to date. The rangers were adamant we had put it in the tree for her, but we hadn't – I think this feat would have been even more difficult for us to achieve than her.

With Tjellers killing such large prey, apart from the time needed to suffocate the animal while it struggled against her lesser weight, unless she had time enough to regain some of her strength before hauling it up the nearest suitable tree, the hyaenas would surely claim it every time. Under more normal conditions and as long as her victim's death throes had not alerted the neighbourhood hyaenas, Tjellers would have had more than enough time, possibly even to open up the carcass and remove the bulky stomach and its contents. The stomach constitutes a substantial proportion of the antelope's total weight and, although not doing this intentionally, the eviscerated carcass would have been far more manageable to hoist into a tree. In her current circumstances, Tjellers was now faced with an almost ever-present threat from her greatest competitor.

Leopards are highly versatile animals, however, and she soon adapted to her new situation. Selecting only the smaller impala from a herd, she would quite literally grab the individual, spin with it still struggling in her jaws, and clamber up the nearest tree with the hyaenas closing in behind her. On a few occasions our hearts were in our mouths as we watched a hyaena jump, as best a hyaena can, and snap at the fast-disappearing meal dangling between our heroine's hind legs. Her back paws were just as accessible to the hyaena's jaws as were parts of the kill.

Some time after our film was completed, on another shoot at Mala Mala, I witnessed just such an event between a male leopard and an arrogant hyaena. The carcass was too heavy for the male to handle; he hung suspended in motion half up the trunk of the tree as the hyaena locked its jaws onto his hind ankle and pulled. Both leopard and carcass were dislodged from the tree and fell on top of the hyaena. No leopard will stand his ground in such a situation, and the male ran off as fast as his wounded leg would carry him.

It is unfortunate for the hyaena that such incidents and sequences such as those documented in our film depict them as vicious, horrible creatures. To the leopard and other animals they may well be formidable opponents, but to typecast them as all bad and highly dangerous, as so many people are prone to do, is simply neither fair nor accurate. We developed a great affection for the spotted hyaena, and if nothing else was happening on a particular night, then the 'spotties', as we liked to call them, were always a constant source of amusement. And they are definitely not vicious and dangerous towards man.

In a natural environment where they have not been exposed to irresponsible human influences, the spotted hyaena presents little threat, day or night. Where lions and leopards are clearly creatures to be treated with the utmost respect and caution, in our experience the truly wild hyaena is totally harmless, even when confronted on foot. It is only those individuals that have been fed by hand on left-over bones and meat through public camp fences that become the problem animals. Losing their natural fear of man and learning to associate people with a source of food, they fast become a threat, demanding the expected handouts.

As with the leopards, we started to recognize specific hyaenas. In particular there were two individuals that we soon got to know quite well: 'Jaws' and 'Lippies'. From what we could make out, they were senior members of two separate clans that held territories overlapping with that of Tjellers. If we were not being trailed at some stage throughout the night by the one, then it was the other. As is typically the case with senior members of a hyaena clan, both were enormous females. With bulging, barrel-like guts they looked as if at any minute they were about to explode from a build up of internal gasses! But their faces were truly their distinguishing features. Jaws had what appeared to be a damaged jaw – it must have been broken at some stage in her past, but had healed well enough for her to survive. Jaws' bottom lip hung away from her jaw, exposing her protruding bottom row of teeth. She was very ugly, but with the passing of time we began to see beyond her physical shortcomings and she endeared herself to us completely.

We first encountered her one day as she lay cooling off from the heat of the day in a pan covered with a green algal scum. Wet and dripping, head partially submerged, she had a decidedly sorry-for-herself look about her. We thought she was nearing her end, but only recently was still seen around the property causing havoc with the leopards.

Lippies likewise had a tear out of her bottom lip, presumably from fighting or squabbling over a carcass with fellow competitors. When feeding on a small carcass things can get quite heated and frantic between hyaenas and it is rather easy to imagine a stray tooth hooking her lip and tearing part of it away. The wound had healed into what looked like a marble-sized wart growing on the end of her bottom lip, slightly off to the side. She was our favourite. She provided us with hours of entertainment through her antics and interactions with the leopards.

About six months into filming, Lippies was followed everywhere she went by what must have been her cub, now a number of months old and capable of hunting and staying with her all night. Naming this little fur ball of trouble was not difficult: he was hopeless and clueless around any kill, and powerless when fighting with fellow siblings. Most of all, his size left him totally insignificant compared to any of the adults in his clan. We called him 'Less'. Lippies and Less, our near constant companions.

As fond as we became of them, however, their regular appearance when we were trying to film the leopards could be very frustrating. Just when something

RICHARD DU TOIT

People often only witness the less appealing aspects of spotted hyaena behaviour, often dismissing them as ugly scavengers. But they are intelligent opportunists and we came to admire the 'spotties' as we called them, and were often witnesses to engaging interaction such as this moment of tenderness between a female and her cub.

NILS KURE

Jaws cools off from the heat of the day in her favourite algae-infested pan.

JAMIE THOM

different and worth filming might have developed with Tjellers and her cubs, these two hyaenas would come blundering in and spoil things. Not to mention all the potential kills they must have upset by rushing in at top speed while Tjellers was cautiously sneaking up on her prey. They had no patience at all. One of the hyaena's hunting techniques is to chase something down and tire it out over a distance until it is unable to run any further. So whenever Tjellers was close enough to her prey to start her stalk, Lippies and Less would also get excited by the near proximity of food and start their chase.

On some evenings, and knowing full well that these two were trailing her, Tjellers would sometimes catch an impala and hand it over to them without any argument. By the way she reacted, one could tell she was not surprised by their sudden appearance to claim her meal, only seconds after the impala's alarm calls had filled the air. Knowing they were now preoccupied, Tjellers would leave the scene immediately and move off in search of another meal for herself. Other leopards we followed during our stay – the Jakkalsdraai male, Trollops and Flockies, amongst others – would all, if their kills were stolen from them, hang around the feeding hyaenas waiting in the wings for any opportunity to snatch something of the carcass back from them. Sometimes Tjellers, if not too desperate for a meal, would also try this, but not often. She would do better to kill again.

Hyaenas love to fight over their meals and Lippies and Less were no exception. Biting at each other's necks they would become so involved in their little tussle that Tjellers, if she was so inclined, was sometimes able to dart in, grab the now half-eaten carcass from under their noses and carry it up the nearest tree before they even realized what was happening. In fact it was frequently the sound of the leopard's claws raking up the bark of the tree that would alert them as to what was going on. Not knowing what the sound was at first, both hyaenas would scuttle off in alarm and in opposite directions before returning to the spot, only then to realize their mistake.

Interestingly, although presumably one of the senior females of a clan, Lippies was seldom seen feeding on a carcass together with other hyaenas, even when distinctly within the area to which we knew her to belong. She would also often kill for herself, and yet very few intruders would try to share in her catch. It was almost as if she was an independent matriarch. We mostly found her around the Tjellahanga River, but twice, in midwinter, we were to find Lippies around Kirkman's Camp at the river crossing, some distance from home, and clearly poaching in another clans' territory. We also saw her on one occasion about the same distance to the north of her core area. Around these periods we were also aware of her absence from Tjellers' territory for some months.

Leopards also seem adept at recognizing specific individuals of other species. For example, for the leopards a hyaena is not just a hyaena, but an individual either stronger or weaker than his fellows or themselves. At first we were only able to discern a hyaena as adult, juvenile or 'big-mommy' (if she was one of the

ROWAN STRETTON

OPPOSITE, ABOVE AND BELOW
Hyaenas are the true comics of the bushveld. As we spent more and more time filming, we came to know the individual hyaenas almost as well as Tjellers (top) must have done.

MILS KURE

CHRIS DAPHNE

ABOVE *The epitome of motherly love. A lioness carries her cub, gently holding the tiny body in her jaws*
OPPOSITE *One of the 'murderers'. The light and shadow cast by the flash seems to add to the menace of the powerful male.*
PHOTOGRAPH: DALE HANCOCK & KIM WOLHUTER

large-stomached, dominant members of the clan). The leopards, on the other hand, and in the few split seconds available to them, would identify the individual as either someone to be reckoned with, or not. Soon we were also adept at distinguishing some of those individuals the leopards considered threats.

For whatever reason, even some of the quite large adult hyaenas were not taken too seriously. But while a leopard might have been reluctant to give up its kill to one of these less threatening individuals, it would not even hesitate before fleeing when catching sight or sound of one of the real bullies of the clan.

If injured in a fight a leopard's chances of survival can be hindered dramatically. This was powerfully demonstrated towards the end of our stay at Mala Mala, when Tjellers was badly injured by a hyaena whilst protecting the newborn Stevie at the lair. She was bitten on one of her back ankles and for weeks was unable to hunt and kill while it healed. It was dire straits for her and her month-old offspring.

Apart from being entertained by their nightly antics in interaction with leopards, the hyaenas did prove quite valuable in what we were able to learn from them. Any aggression on the part of a leopard is usually more show than intent. An experienced hyaena will ignore a leopard's show of force and can generally intimidate the leopard into standing down. This observation proved useful when filming from out of the vehicle. As accepting of us as she was, occasionally Tjellers would react adversely to our presence on foot and charge, but by emulating the nonchalance of the hyaenas and ignoring her display we avoided otherwise potentially dangerous situations. We also learnt that when her 'hackles were up' it was best to avoid eye contact to settle her as soon as possible. To stare at her in such a situation was to incite sure trouble. No leopard likes to be stared at, even in the most ordinary of circumstances.

One morning, after an entire night of sitting with Tjellers on a kill, she had shown no indication to us that she was at all concerned with our presence. Then, when the first game-drive vehicle approached her at the base of the tree, she rushed it. Six to eight pairs of intent eyes all boring into hers as they approached was too much for her to handle, and she must have felt threatened.

One of the stronger sequences in the film is that of the saga of the newborn lion cub. We found the little cub abandoned by its wounded mother soon after sunset in some open grassland at the edge of some bush. The cub was still a bit wet and probably only a couple of hours old. The mother was lying up about 20 metres away, blood still dripping from her vagina. The little cub was calling continuously for her, but she showed no interest in nursing it and often snarled when it called. An hour later, after dark and with the cub still calling, the Jakkalsdraai male leopard arrived and went over to the crying cub. Nervous at his approach the lioness jumped up and moved off. Her reaction also unnerved him and he too left the area. Staying with the lion cub, we listened to its calls become more and more desperate

NILS KURE

ABOVE *A lioness has treed a leopard and its kill, and now she worries at the smaller cat, intent on distracting it to the point that it might drop its meal into her waiting jaws.*
OPPOSITE *A lion devours a male impala.*

for attention, attention we knew would never come – at least not from its mother, who was now hobbling off in the other direction.

Several hours later Tjellers arrived on the scene, also drawn by the unusual cries. Approaching cautiously, she sniffed the cub all over, licked its backside in a typical grooming fashion and then sniffed it some more. Hyaenas also began to gather nearby, typically squealing and giggling as each newcomer greeted the others and licked at their genitals. Tjellers picked up the cub as if to try to leave the scene with it, but then turned to listen to the building excitement of the growing hyaena horde and put it down again. All the time she was very much on edge and behaving, in our interpretation, very protectively towards the lion cub.

Newborn impala fawns are said to remain scentless for the first few days of their lives to avoid detection from predators whilst left hidden by their mothers in long grass. We have even witnessed a leopard almost walk right over a day-old fawn without noticing it. Could the lion cub have been unidentifiable to the

DALE HANCOCK

JAMES WAKELIN

A most humorous event. Unlike leopards, lions are for the most part out of their league in trees. But this does not always stop them from venturing along a high branch with great trepidation to steal a leopard's kill.

CHRIS DAPHNE

A lioness and her cubs on the alert. Such nervousness is often displayed at the approach of intruding males. Newcomers, upon 'taking over' a pride, may well kill the offspring of their rivals and then mate with the females of the pride to sire their own progeny.

leopard for similar reasons? Could the cries of the cub in some way have excited her maternal instincts? A hyaena approached. Tjellers snarled at it and it moved off. And then she too moved off, leaving the lion cub behind, calling all the more rapidly and with renewed vigour. The same hyaena then circled, came in, picked the cub up, shook it and carried it off. It killed the cub, promptly dropped it, and left, not showing any interest in eating it.

Tjellers seemingly wanting to adopt the cub was in itself very interesting, but what makes it even more so is that only two weeks before, she was seen showing no compunction in biting the heads off two serval kittens. Some time after this she also chased down and killed an African wild cat.

To live and work in the wild one learns to accept such ruthlessness towards rival predators as being in the natural order of things. But having said that, the killing of a lioness by two dominant male lions, another strong sequence in *Beauty and the Beasts,* was something else. To us this seemed totally unnecessary and from that day on we called the culprits 'the murderers'.

Some days after having abandoned her newborn cub, we followed the lioness as she limped her way towards the rest of her small pride that we could hear calling some distance to the north. Her injury, now a week old, seemed to be getting better as she was favouring the damaged foot less and less. With little or nothing to eat since her mishap, however, she tired quickly. Between frequent rest periods she would call to her pride, which only responded infrequently. For a while a small group of hyaenas harassed her, delighting in her inability to chase them as she would normally do. For about 10 minutes they taunted her before moving on to satisfy other, more pressing needs such as their hunger.

Now exhausted by the extra energy needed to keep the hyaenas at bay, she remained lying down and soon her pride ran in. Presumably they had heard the excitement of the hyaenas harassing her and her distressed growls in response. Notwithstanding the moral support arriving a little late, she appeared overjoyed to see her pride mates again. She was the senior member of the group, and said to be mother of the other four sub-adult lions that at that stage made up the River Rocks pride.

All lay down and called in unison, and without any warning two adult males ran in at full charge. The entire pride scattered, catching us off guard and leaving us both standing and a little bewildered by the speed at which it had all happened. About 300 metres to the south we heard the strained cries and roaring of lions in battle and we knew then that the two males had caught the injured female. Rushing down to the scene of the commotion we came across both males lying on the struggling female. The one had her by the head and was crushing her scull, while the other, not quite as aggressive as his partner, was tearing at her stomach. Slowly her guttural growls diminished to a mere gurgle, and five minutes later she was dead. The Toulon males, as they were known, had just killed a female with whom they had at least occasionally previously met up.

It was a cold winter's night shortly after midnight when it happened, and after it was over a deathly quiet settled over the bush. Not even an insect was to be heard. The whole place seemed to be in mourning. As it happened, that evening some rangers were out on a transport run escorting guests from a late-night party at Main Camp back to Kirkman's. After we had recovered somewhat from the shock and dramatic impact of what we had just filmed, Kim called them on the radio to fill them in and could hardly speak. I know that the events of that night are a memory that will live with us both for quite some time.

Again Lex Hes in his *Leopards of Londolozi* offers an interesting comparison. Although not involving lions, as in our experience, Lex sites an incident involving leopards: 'To this day it remains a mystery why a male leopard should have killed a female, especially on reaching sexual maturity. Possibly, she was coming into oestrus and this had attracted the male. The close physical contact during mating is an aggressive affair. Then there was the possibility that the male had perceived Sticknyawo's disability as a sign of weakness and had attacked her.' The parallels between the two events are almost hauntingly similar, but nonetheless difficult to explain. At least not to any satisfaction.

DALE HANCOCK

ABOVE AND BELOW *A contest over food between Tjellers and one of her arch rivals. Although such closely related predators (both belong to the genus* Panthera*), lions and leopards are implacable enemies.*

Nils Kure, then head ranger and now manager of Mala Mala, has to my mind best interpreted the possible reasons for the lions' actions: 'Violence in lions is well documented, and it is a long established fact that new males in an area will kill the small cubs. This has an effect of bringing the females into season again, enabling the recently dominant males to mate with them and thereby pass their genes on. As such it is probably a desirable effect, but maybe an incidental consequence of other factors ... The pointlessness of this deed [the abovementioned murder] was initially hard to fathom, until I gave some thought to how male lions make the acquaintance of females in areas which are new to them. For the first month or few, there is a good deal of chasing and of running away. The females keep their distance, until eventually each party becomes reconciled to the other and finally associate on amicable terms. Young cubs are killed, therefore, not because they are not the issue of the newcoming males' loins, but because, being smaller, they cannot run as well as can the adults and are thereby caught. The same fate might apply to an adult female who, owing to injury or circumstance, is caught by males that do not know her (at least not well) and, as a consequence of their very nature, attack her with a fatal viciousness.'

DALE HANCOCK

There was one time in particular when Tjellers demonstrated an unexpected and considerable show of force in her own right, but with a much happier ending. Shortly after giving a scrub hare to her cubs to play with, the same pride of lionesses as mentioned in the previous incident arrived unannounced and the cubs fled in panic, nearly to be caught by one of the passing lionesses. Tjellers, in somewhat of a panic too, promptly charged at one of the innocent lionesses that

NILS KURE

had already passed. The lioness turned around, astounded, and stood staring in amazement at the arrogance of this lightweight leopard.

Weight for weight the lioness was nearly four times heavier than Tjellers and towered over her much smaller adversary, just feet from her nose. Unsure of this very unusual situation the lioness took a pace towards our leopard. Now, as if reconsidering the wisdom of her brave charge, Tjellers flipped onto her side in submission, much as when greeting the Jakkalsdraai male after a long absence. She was now totally at the mercy of the lioness. Our hearts were in our throats. Leopard still hissing and forelimbs angled up at the lioness, the larger cat thought better of the situation and backed down.

Released from her trapped pose Tjellers fled. By that stage the cubs were safely ensconced up a nearby marula tree. We did film the event, but as it all happened so unexpectedly, Kim was rushed to start rolling and the shot was sadly unusable.

During another lion/leopard interaction in which a sub-adult male lion had approached the base of the tree in which Four was feeding, he was met with a rather unpleasant reception. Frozen at the kill, Four watched the lion saunter up to the tree until standing directly below. Staring up at both cub and carcass and possibly contemplating whether he should exert himself to climb up and take it from her, Four lost all control of her bladder, the contents of which cascaded down onto the face staring vacantly up at her. This proved decisive in persuading the lion not to climb the tree and, with as much dignity as possible under the circumstances, he sauntered off into the night, snorting and shaking his head.

Surprisingly few people realize just how adept lions are at climbing; even trees with few branches and near vertical trunks. We recorded and witnessed a number of such impressive events. Taking a carcass up a tree may be surety against hyaenas forcefully taking food from leopards, but the same cannot necessarily be said regarding lions. Yes, they are comparatively clumsy and out of sorts in a tree, but capable, nonetheless, of reaching almost the same heights and extremities as most leopards. Knowing this, the leopard will almost always abandon the tree, later if not sooner, sometimes nearly into the jaws of the remaining pride members below. The leopard cub that is killed in the film by lions was caught in a similar fashion. Desperate to escape the oncoming pair of lionesses, it panicked and ran up a spindly red bushwillow tree that bent under its weight and began to droop. Hearing the movement, the lionesses walked over to the tree, one jumping up onto it and adding her weight to the already straining trunk. With this the cub lost its nerve and bailed out, only to fall at the feet of the second beast. The hapless young leopard was mauled to death almost instantly.

Although most of the threats to leopards come from lions and hyaenas, some other interesting adversaries made a few cameo appearances. In one instance the thief of the leopard's kill was a two-and-a-half metre crocodile, which took advantage of a kill that Flockies had made close to the Sand River. Usually an

PIETER DROSS

OPPOSITE *Two of Tjellers' near constant companions grooming themselves at the start of yet another night of harassing the female leopard as she hunted.*
ABOVE *Lions investigating a porcupine. Lions will kill and eat porcupines, but tackling such prickly prey has its risks; many a lion has suffered serious infection as a result of being stabbed by the formidable spines.*

avid defender of his meals, there was no argument from Flockies on this occasion and he wisely left the crocodile to its purloined spoils.

Although not witness to it ourselves, we were also told of a fascinating confrontation between a leopard and a large python over the rights to a carcass. Not altogether unusual for a snake of its size, the python had managed to catch an adult duiker. Attracted by the antelope's plaintive cries, a nearby leopard came to investigate. For quite some time the leopard sat back and watched with interest as the python eventually crushed its prey with a few well-placed coils.

Approaching a little closer the leopard was struck at by the python and kept at bay. Ever patient, the leopard decided to back off once more and observe for a while longer. Lying comfortably in the shade of a nearby bush he watched as the snake stretched its jaws and proceeded to swallow the duiker whole. This took some while to achieve but, patiently biding its time, the leopard waited for the snake to properly commit itself to its meal before strolling up to it and giving it one solid whack on the head with its paw. Stunned, and suddenly having lost its appetite, the python quickly disgorged what it had so far managed to force down its throat, presenting it to the leopard who was quick to pick up the meal and run off with it. This time there was no arguing with the leopard.

TABLE FIVE	***LEOPARD / HYAENA INTERACTIONS***
interactions over carcasses (average of one every three days)	134
interactions without the presence of a carcass	27
leopard's intended kill taken before animal properly dead	17
leopard's kill taken after animal properly dead and not having been treed	65
leopard successful in treeing carcass before approaching hyaena can steal it	31
leopard unsuccessful in treeing carcass before approaching hyaena can steal it	4
carcass taken from leopard before leopard has chance to feed	29
leopard steals back part of carcass	10
leopard leaves carcass to hyaena without any defence	47
hyaena waiting at base of tree and benefiting from dropped carcass	13
leopard and hyaena engage in conflict	14
caught impala gets away from leopard and hyaena	3
leopard hangs around a hyaena kill	2
leopard waits around after kill stolen	14
interactions involving Lippies	20

TABLE SIX	***LEOPARD/LION INTERACTIONS***
number of leopard kills taken by lions	15
number of leopard kills discovered by lion but not retrieved by them	7
leopard/lion interaction without motivation of food	6
leopard/lion interaction with kill finally consumed by lion or leopard	2

OPPOSITE *Lions will squabble amongst themselves over food, no matter the location. Here two individuals engage each other, seemingly oblivious to their precarious clawhold.*

DALE HANCOCK

RICHARD DU TOIT

Mother warthog and her month-old piglets.

CHAPTER FIVE

Wart alert

DALE HANCOCK

Warthogs have been unflatteringly described by authorities as 'incarnations of hideous dreams' … or as 'the most astonishing objects that have disgraced nature' … and while they may not have the grace of an impala or the dignity of a lion, they are an integral and very interesting part of the spectrum of African wildlife.

Reay H N Smithers
The Mammals of the Southern African Subregion

PIETER DROS

Stevie, now a young adult, sniffs intently at a stalk. Leopards glean a large part of their information about the world around them, and who they are sharing it with, from their acute sense of smell.

Hunched over on a stool, head propped up against the rheostats for the lights illuminating the burrow, half conscious and deep in contemplation about nothing in particular, a faint wheezing squeak muffled by the cloth partitioning between man and beast sounded the alert that at last something was happening. 'Our' warthog was giving birth.

Night after night for nigh on a month we had stood guard, peering every 10 to 15 minutes through the little window we had made into the sleeping sow's haven, waiting and waiting, seemingly endlessly for one of the few predictable and scripted sequences to our film. The only action on these long evenings was the occasional, ever so slight movement of the pregnant warthog to regain her comfort, and a few heavy sighs; either from our subject or a tiring observer.

PETER CHADWICK

A warthog family, or sounder, secure in its burrow. Piglets are confined to the burrow for their first month or more before they venture out.

For a while, in my somewhat sleep-deprived state, I didn't even register what was happening. It all felt strangely like a dream. These faint new sounds so obviously different from anything else we had heard these past weeks seemed almost to come from deep within my subconscious. Finally the penny dropped. Fumbling in half shock, half excitement, I pulled the black velvet curtain aside to witness the birth struggles of one of Mala Mala's newest residents. Snatching a glance at my watch I noticed it was 10 to one, only eight minutes since I had last checked on the pregnant sow. Looking back through the hole again I noticed another small, pink-grey body stumble out from behind the much larger bulk of the adult female, still seemingly fast asleep, although now in the throes of giving birth. It transpired that one piglet had already been born and

KIM WOLHUTER

The barred owl is a common Lowveld resident, where it is found mostly in thick riverine forests.

it was now number two on the way. The sound I had been hearing was in fact the first piglet stumbling around, trying to find a teat on which to suckle.

Warthogs usually give birth to some four young each year (sometimes as many as six), so another two were hopefully still to come. Exploding from our observation pit I called to Kim who was sleeping only a few metres away in his vehicle. Within seconds we were both back in the pit where all the equipment was ready and waiting to start filming. By this stage the second piglet was also up and about on its legs searching and squealing for milk. Both had been born within about 15 minutes, so the third and, if we were to be lucky, the fourth couldn't be far behind. But by two-thirty things still had not developed any further. Both piglets had finally drunk their fill and scrambled together up onto mom's stomach to sleep. Where were the other two expected newcomers?

As usual we began to think of all the possible explanations for this frustrating turn of events. Murphy's law seems to take great delight in following a wildlife film maker around. When we first started to work with this female in order to habituate her to our presence, we had noted how old and wrinkled she looked. This was actually one of the reasons for chosing her as our main warthog star; she had such wonderful character compared to the other, younger-looking individuals. But, we now began to regret our choice. As a distinctly ageing sow, we began to conject that she probably no longer had the ability to produce a full litter. After all the time, effort and a considerable amount of money, it seemed we were going to miss our chance at a sequence we thought we had in the bag!

With the initial adrenaline rush now wearing off, by a quarter to four both of us started to doze again. For some strange reason, I decided to take one last drowsy peak beyond the curtain, and I noticed a tiny, wet nose easing its way out from under the female's tail. Some two hours after the other pair had rushed into the world, the runt was now making his appearance. We were saved! Not only that, but this third and the last of the piglets to be born was far and away the most comical of the three. This poor chap could not break free from his umbilical cord and spent quite some time trying to untangle himself. Pulling with all his might to reach a teat only inches from his nose, the umbilical cord would stretch out taught behind him. His back legs now raised off the ground, the front two would scrape and skid on the burrow floor searching for traction. We were tempted to name him 'Dunlop'. For ages the 'bungee cord' would stretch and contract, throwing him off balance and onto his face, until eventually it broke.

Wobbly, exhausted and no doubt frustrated, our hero stumbled for a teat dripping with milk in front of his stubby and by now quite dusty nose. Venting his pent up frustration, he pulled at the teat until we thought it would compete with the umbilical cord for length. How it was not painful for the sow we do not know, but she just seemed to sleep on through it all, every so often sending out a reassuring grunt to her young that resounded and reverberated impressively within the amplifying effect of the burrow walls.

To film the birth sequence we had excavated a vertical shaft from the centre of the termite mound, in which the burrow was situated, down to the level of the warthog's chamber. Our hole had to be big enough to house both of us with all our equipment (radio included for those long nights of waiting). The side through which we peered was held back by planks in which we had cut a hole just big enough for our lenses to poke through. We used to joke to all our visitors that this had to be the happiest warthog in the bush: she had security lights doubling as internal heating, piped in music, neighbourhood watch, pest control and possibly even a wet nurse if needed. The only thing she did not have was meals-on-wheels. We, on the other hand, had to suffer all the tampans and other crawlies that used to visit our side of the hole throughout the night.

The mother we called 'Wiggins', a name made up mainly from a play on the words warthog and pig, making 'Wig'. The three piglets too held derivatives of her name. We called them 'Wi' (pronounced 'Wee', for small), 'Ig' (which suited the clown), and 'Gin', the runt and only male of the group, after his somewhat drunken, unstable appearance on coming into this world. Again we were ridiculed for our provocative choice of names, confirming the effectiveness of our selection.

Warthog piglets spend a little over a week entirely holed up underground with their mothers. Seldom does the sow even venture out to feed, and when she does it is of brief duration and within a very short radius of the burrow. The piglets will usually huddle together in a heap, shivering with fear at the furthest reaches from the entrance, waiting for mom to return. As their nervousness increases at having been abandoned, they try to climb on top of each other in the absence of their mother's platform, and a high-pitched squealing-squabble ensues, each trying to reach the pinnacle of the mound. Predictably, Gin always ended up at the bottom of the heap. When Wiggins returned to her brood, grunting deeply, Wi, Ig and Gin would respond with much squeaking and bouncing around the hole in excitement.

In their second week the three piglets began to venture out. Wiggins would lie with her head protruding from the entrance and her backside still half blocking the hole. Soon the piglets were squeezing past her flanks and out into the big, wide world. The leading piglet, however, would frequently lose its nerve, and would make a few hasty retreats on the way out, in the process reversing into its siblings bringing up the rear.

After much advancing and retreating in the ranks they all emerged alongside mom's head, somewhat bewildered at the brightness and size of everything around them. Alarmed by this new experience, yet placated by mom's close proximity, they darted around outside in a stop-start manner, colliding with everything in their paths in their haste. Sniffing at as much as they could within a few feet of Wiggins' head and tentatively chewing on their first blades of rich, green grass, the adventurous trio soon disappeared back into the comforting depths of the family burrow. Enough excitement for one day!

NILS KURE

The leopard usually looks its best for photographs in the twilight hours, or in overcast conditions.

In time the family group would move away from the burrow on a feeding trip, the distance and duration of which increased day by day. All the other sounders (the collective term for a family of warthogs) were initially kept well at bay by the sows, but with the increasing inquisitiveness of the piglets, some of these sounders soon amalgamated into larger family groups, the sows of which were presumably closely related. Individual females, and some newly with piglets, that we surmised were immigrants to the area, and thus not closely related to any of the other resident females, were never well received. On first sight, they were always chased away, the piglets sometimes scattering in the confusion as their mothers charged around, looking like miniature tanks on their short, stocky legs.

The piglets from these larger groupings would spend protracted periods chasing each other in play about the veld in an almost insane manner. Never at anything but full pace, the whole group of up to eight little bodies would rush back and forth past their peacefully grazing mothers with seemingly endless energy. Eventually, and almost on command, all would rush up to their respective parents and, gathered around her hind legs, quench their now serious thirsts. The sow seemed almost to take a sensual pleasure from this suckling. Breaking from her constant feeding, she would raise her head, eyes half shut, and stand gently swaying under the rocking motion of the suckling piglets tugging at her teats beneath her belly. Eventually the sow would take a few steps forward to resume her feeding and the piglets would be forced to break free and continue their explorations. The runt, of course, would hang on for those last few swallows, dragged along and trampled beneath mom's feet until reluctantly falling free.

Throughout the shooting of our film we were asked many a time: 'Why a film on leopards and warthogs? What is the connection?' Well, the connection was in reality more one of no connection at all, but rather one of complete contrast. The leopard is a carnivore, the warthog an omnivore (they will also eat carrion). The leopard is indisputably beautiful; the warthogs are just plain ugly to most people, although we came to regard them as very loveable and attractive friends. And, of course, the one is a predator, while the other is prey.

With our producer's original film concept being specifically one about leopards and warthogs, we needed somehow to link both species throughout our story. Our clearest link from the start between such dramatically differing animals was the potential to record an encounter between the two. It didn't really matter what sort of encounter, just so long as they came together and interacted in some way so that we could film it and bring our two separate stories together.

It should be obvious to most people that we would have been looking for a warthog kill from our leopards, hopefully so as to tie in the two species' stories. But the connection between the two tales had to be more than just that. We wanted the two dramas to run parallel, linking back and forth with motivation

OPPOSITE *The Jakkalsdraai male alert to something a little way off. Rather in the manner of a suricate, leopards will very occasionally raise themselves into this unusual posture, presumably to get a better sighting of prey hidden by the long grass or some other obstacle.*

JAMES RAWDON

CHRIS DAPHNE

The respected adult male warthog. With their sharp tusks and considerable bulk, male warthogs are by no means easy prey for leopards.

throughout the length of the film. We wanted, wherever possible, to compare the two animals directly – highlighting the differences and, surprisingly sometimes, the similarities between them. We intended to illustrate the dangers faced by both as they grew from infants to adults.

Their social structures should have differed, yet comparisons remained. For example, techniques of defense one would have thought to have been quite contrasting, yet in subtle ways were not; territories were a mutual concern to both leopards and warthogs, but with the warthogs such issues as land tenure were more complicated than the simple, almost one-animal-one-territory of the leopards; diet was in some cases even identical, as warthogs were seen at times, although rarely, to eat both scrub hares and buffalo carrion. How and when they went about reproducing became a very interesting comparison; and so cross-referencing went on. Whatever the link, we would try to make it. But we still wanted to be faithful to, and illustrate the unique characters within each group, and most importantly the humor we saw in so many of the events witnessed.

NILS KURE

Twilight is when most predators wake to start the night's prowling. Here Tjellers begins to stir from her daytime resting place in the high branch of a marula tree.

Unfortunately for us, Mala Mala and the whole Lowveld region had over the past few years weathered a heavy drought, and one of the species most affected by this deprivation was the warthog. Numbers had plummeted to desperately low levels, leaving fewer and fewer opportunities for interaction with predators. There just weren't enough of them around anymore.

We followed Flockies, the acknowledged warthog specialist, for months on end, hoping he would find one of the last survivors, but to no avail. The Styx lion pride was found digging one morning at a warthog burrow in the north, but they too gave up on their efforts before anything came of the event. Time was running out and we still didn't have that crucial link. However, in documenting the more subtle elements of the pigs' lives, and working with the last individuals remaining around the 'oasis' of Mala Mala Main Camp, we were at least having some order of success.

As with the birth season, the warthogs logically have a specific season in which they mate, and at Mala Mala this is around May. At the commencement of the mating season, the sow will urinate frequently to advertise her readiness.

KIM WOLHUTER

ABOVE *'Stumpy' is one of the warthogs born during the early summer when we were filming* Beauty and the Beasts, *and is now a large adult male easily identified from a crowd by the loss of a major part of his 'aerial'.*
OPPOSITE *Warthogs engaging in the rituals of courtship and mating.*
PHOTOGRAPH: PETER CHADWICK

In the area we had chosen to concentrate our efforts, best suited to following the most warthogs, we had not usually seen any adult males. The only males were those sub-adults from the previous year's litters that still hung around in loose family groups. Now there seemed to be a flood of potential suitors. All the usual residents to the area were by this stage well habituated to our presence, but these newcomers, the large adult males, were not so sure of us. This led to much humour, and it is here that the fun and games started.

Each female would reach her readiness to mate at slightly delayed times from one to the other and, in so doing would attract all the interest from the available males at her particular time. This would include all adult males, irrespective of size or age group. Even the barely post-pubescent year-and-a-half sub-adults took part in the contest. The largest of the males, weighing in at a good 80 kilograms plus, would all vie competitively for her attentions, strutting about on fully stretched legs, bristling with strained hopes and expectations.

These congregations of pigs all around one family group were easy to find, but as soon as we approached to start filming, all the males that had not become habituated to our presence would run away and circle us in the wings, frantic with frustration. The resident sub-adult males, fully habituated and possessed with these first-time sexual urges, couldn't believe their luck at the sudden disappearance of the big heavies. Not wasting a second, these youngsters would rush in and, dispensing with the formalities, would mount the females almost immediately. Not having been brought to a complete standstill by way of the usual foreplay from the experienced adult males, the females would carry on walking around with the ecstatic first-timers riding along behind, unsuccessful, but blissfully happy at the lack of competition.

The large males soon began to accept our presence, however, and, enraged by the arrogance of their younger fellows, would charge in to claim their right. With the females as such strong motivation, all the males soon settled and, ignoring us, went about their business (or pleasure) in the normal fashion. The sub-adults' unnatural monopoly of the situation was over and we could begin to document things on film with accuracy.

In contrast to the tense and physical approach of the leopards to mating, and the fear and uncertainty that it created in their cubs, the warthogs were quite another story. To begin with, the male comes up to the female, champing his strange love sonnet to her as he follows her around. With tail half cocked, the male struts along behind, resting his drooling chin on the female's back and rump. Eventually, after playing hard to get for long enough, the female stops and backs up to the male, allowing him to mount her for the first time.

Of course, as with the leopard cubs, this is the first time the young, six- to seven-month-old piglets have seen mother and her suitors in the act of mating. It is probably the first time they have seen her doing anything much other than eat, wallow, or chase off one of her peers. So to them the sights and sounds of

DALE HANCOCK

Evening, and the heat of the bushveld day eases. With seeming reluctance, a leopard opens its eyes to face the night ahead.

such activity are intriguing. An audience of up to eight piglets can at any one time be seen gathered around the engaged pair, sniffing and nudging them.

With the approach of spring and with the new season's piglets on their way, there were a few changes taking place in warthog society. Now, with only a few weeks to go before the birth of their new litters, the females would start insisting on sleeping alone in their burrows at night. The previous year's broods, which had religiously followed their mothers around for the past 350-odd days, were now faced with a new reality. As a tightly knit group came to search out a hole to sleep in for the night, the year-old members of the family were forced to find their own, separate burrow. Reversing into her burrow, the pregnant female would stop in the entrance, so preventing the others from following. Also, the

DALE HANCOCK

juvenile pigs would turn and begin to back into the burrow only to be shoved out again by their mother with a loud huff and with plenty of dust tossed out from within. Confused, the young pigs would nervously go off in search of a nearby vacant hole in which to spend the night, hoping to join up with their mother again the next morning.

Each respective sounder seemed to have a number of favourite holes and would rotate between them every few days. Usually, as the afternoon drew on, the adult female leading the group would head for her chosen burrow for that night and feed in the immediate vicinity of the entrance before finally going below. Her timeous arrival in the area was presumably to ensure her being there early enough to fend off any other female with similar intentions for the same hole.

Now, however, we were surprised at how late the females headed for home. With twilight heavy on the horizon they would make straight for their chosen

ABOVE *The event for which we had waited so long – a leopard zeros in on its prey.*
OVERLEAF *Warthogs, even young ones, are never easy targets for leopards. We witnessed an encounter in which a young male leopard was bested by a year-old female warthog.*

PHOTOGRAPH: DALE HANCOCK

CHRIS DAPHNE

Even against a pride of lions a warthog can put up a good fight. In one gruesome encounter, we watched as lions took more than 20 minutes to subdue a warthog.

burrow and enter immediately. On the first few evenings the female would allow her family to follow, but with her delivery more imminent, she then began preventing them from doing so, forcing them to run around in near darkness in search of another, alternative lodging. One of the sub-adult females of a group we followed extensively became wise to her mother's intentions and, knowing which burrow they were headed for, would dart off ahead of the group to duck in before the adult arrived. This was not tolerated and the adult would descend headfirst into the burrow and, amid much squealing, unceremoniously evict the insolent youngster from the hole.

Twilight is when the hunter is most active, and this is when the leopard comes into its own. Fresh from his day-long respite and alert to any new potential, a young male leopard eyed one of these nervous little clusters of swine, scurrying about indecisively, not knowing which way to go and straining to see their way in the fading light. Ignoring the usual need for stealth, the leopard rushed in on the warthogs and pounced on the slowest member of the group. Probably one of the most memorable things about a warthog kill is the noise that accompanies it. With a blood-curdling squeal audible for many miles, the warthog bucked and writhed under the weight of her adversary.

Although an adult male warthog can weigh as much as, if not more than his leopard counterpart, this warthog was only a year-old female, substantially smaller than her adversary and yet holding her own. Remaining on her stocky little legs, she eventually managed to break free and drag herself towards a previously unused aardvark burrow, diving headfirst into its protective depths. Without even a developed pair of tusks with which to defend herself, she had, through sheer tenacity, managed to save her hide!

It has always been strongly believed that warthogs always reverse into their burrows, even when retreating in great haste to escape the attentions of a dangerous predator. With our warthogs, however, we were surprised to find that this was not the case. There were still some instances when they would turn before backing into their burrows, but they would mostly just barge straight in, head first. There was always ample room for them to turn around inside and come back out headfirst, without having to reverse into the burrow.

Even though we had such great difficulty in documenting a leopard/warthog interaction, there were a few game drives that witnessed chance sightings of warthogs being killed. Being unpredictable encounters, we were unable to get there to document them, but we were kept well abreast of developments over the radio.

A particularly gruesome event took place when the River Rocks pride caught a large male warthog in a donga off F-bend Open Area. The typical piercing squealing could be clearly heard over the radios as the rangers gave their at-the-scene updates as to what was happening, and directions to the other guest-laden vehicles trying to get there. The 'hog took over 20 minutes to die and vented his terror in voice the entire time. Unable to strangle him around his substantial neck, and to avoid his enormous tusks, the lions literally started to eat the warthog alive. Only the combined weight of four lions was enough to keep the struggling warthog from making good his escape. Not even the most hardened of rangers could have taken any pleasure at this grisly sighting.

Another unexpected link between leopard and warthog came with the death of the leopard cub in the far northeast corner of the reserve. Rangers on their game drives had reported that some lions had killed the unfortunate youngster and we set off in haste to record whatever happened next. We knew it was likely that the mother of the cub would come back to look for the infant in the hope that it might have survived the attack, and we wanted to be there when she returned. As it happened she made her appearance in the early hours of the morning, many hours after the lions had cleared off. After investigating the mauled carcass for about 10 minutes, the mother leopard then abandoned it for good. Whether she would have returned for it later in the day to feed off the carcass in the macabre fashion documented on a few similar occassions in the past, we will never know, for a much stranger event happened in its stead.

An hour or two after sunrise a family of warthogs came shuffling through the bush. Initially unconcerned, they soon picked up the scent, either of the leopard cub's carcass, or the lions from the previous night. Sniffing the air with caution they eventually closed in on the stiff body of the young leopard cub. As mentioned earlier, warthogs are not the mere herbivores most believe them to be. Carrion presents an opportunistic meal and we had, on two previous occasions, witnessed warthogs devouring, with much relish and gusto, newly dead scrub hare carcasses they had found lying under a bush.

The leopard cub was not much bigger than a scrub hare and we wondered what they might do with it. The adult female warthog, clearly not happy with the scent of this unusual find, crept in at full stretch to sniff and test the seemingly lifeless form. It showed all the signs of being harmless and a potential meal, yet her senses must have been on full alert, screaming alarm at her. She took a testing bite at the cub's ear and jumped back. 'Did it move, or was it just her imagination?' She tried again and, getting a little braver, wedged a tusk under the body as if to persuade it to move if still alive. Still nothing. With final resolve she gave it an almighty toss which no live beast could have ignored and in the process terrified herself into thinking that it was now following her in hot pursuit. The family of warthogs disappeared into the distance. With their flags amast, stiff and taut and stretched up and over their backs, they sought to escape the attentions of their unknown and unseen pursuer.

A little later a hyaena found the carcass and devoured it.

TABLE SEVEN

ANIMALS KILLED BY LEOPARD AT MALA MALA
impala
duiker
steenbok
reedbuck
kudu (young)
bushbuck
scrub hare
spring hare (only sighting)
Civet
serval (kittens) – not eaten
genet – not eaten
African wild cat – not eaten
monkey
giraffe (young)
warthog
tree squirrel
mice
Swainson's francolin
crested francolin
Coqui francolin
yellow-billed hornbill
quail
korhaan (black-bellied and red-crested)
python – uncertain (possibly carrion)

TABLE EIGHT

ANIMALS CAUGHT/FOUND BUT NOT KILLED BY LEOPARD AT MALA MALA
terrapin
tortoise
lion

DALE HANCOCK

Tjellers makes a kill. So much of the leopard's life is only revealed at night. We have learnt to appreciate the benefits of nocturnal film making.

CHAPTER SIX

Action, lights, camera!

PETER CHADWICK

The speed and focused fury of a leopard attack is bewildering. But behind it is a seemingly choreographed moment of poise and majesty that only the technique and skill of wildlife photographers can truly capture.

Anthony Hall-Martin
Cats of Africa

PIETER DROS

Stevie, as an adult, struggles with her impressive trophy – an adult male impala.

The preceding quote from respected zoologist and author Anthony Hall-Martin is taken from his collaborative book with wildlife artist, Paul Bosman. He continues: 'One particular sequence filmed recently at the Mala Mala Game Reserve in South Africa [the climatic sequence towards the end of *Beauty and the Beasts*] revealed this more vividly than I can ever recall seeing before. The young leopard, only recently forced by her mother to fend for herself, needed to make a kill. Her hunting technique lacked the consummate ability and confidence of a more mature animal, but determination and a measure of desperation drove her on.

'The camera crew, equally determined to follow her fortunes and to film her first success, tracked her as best they could. Whilst cautiously making her way through the woodland undergrowth, the leopard came upon a small herd of impala, but not cautiously enough, and in a moment the skittish antelope were dodging and leaping through the bush in a flurry of hooves and tawny flanks, presenting an impossible confusion of targets for the young, inexperienced hunter. As

ROWAN STRETTON

The ultimate conquest. A 40kg leopard struggles with a 65kg kudu. It is moments like these for which wildlife film makers will wait years. And then it's over in the flash of an eye.

luck would have it, however, a fully grown male came charging out of the gloom straight towards her. In the drama of slow motion that is part of the modern film-maker's repertoire, the leopard uncoiled out of the grass to meet her quarry. At the moment of impact, both animals were at least a metre off the ground, the force of the collision cartwheeling them through the air in a balletic arc. As they hit the earth, the leopard's jaws had somehow found their target, but still, the powerful male impala managed to struggle on and victory for the cat seemed far from assured. Within a few paces, however, the antelope faltered and minutes later the leopard, chest still heaving, lay triumphantly by her first successful kill.

'I have been privy to many moments of high drama in the bush, and like most of us with a penchant for such things, I have witnessed many more, albeit vicariously, on video and film. For me, however, the scene just described was unlike any other, a true celebration of both the cameraman's skill and uncanny anticipation, and the supreme athleticism and courage of the leopard.'

NILS KURE

ABOVE *The drama of high action sequences are only truly effective if also carefuly countered with contrasting moments of sensitivity.* **OPPOSITE** *Much of what we strive for is to bring authenticity and believability to our films, the elusive '2-shot' – sequences in which all the characters are visible within the same frame – are all important. Without them, events appear contrived rather than real.*

PHOTOGRAPH: DALE HANCOCK

It is no longer sufficient only to document wild animals' lives when making a wildlife documentary. It is also imperative that the images presented to one's audience are as visually stimulating as possible. This requires a great deal of both technical and artistic skill, a detailed instinct for the potential behaviour of one's subject, and an interminable determination to hang in there, sometimes through long periods of comparative boredom.

Gone are the days when a film maker can simply train a camera on a wildlife spectacle through a long telephoto lens, turn it on and hope to record images capable of captivating a 21st-century audience. The visual literacy of people the world round is today incredibly well developed, with the younger generations having been weaned on a barrage of images from such stations as MTV, not to mention the astounding special effects used in movies as wide ranging as *Star Wars* to *Jurassic Park*. Likewise, blue-chip wildlife movie making has to keep up. Detailed editing techniques, the use of big, intimate, full screen close-ups, and well-structured stories with carefully placed climaxes, anticlimaxes and comic relief are all important considerations.

Wildlife behaviour through evolution changes at an almost painfully slow rate, but how we present the scenes of what these animals are about from year to year needs regular reassessment. In keeping with this, we believe it is important to live with one's subjects rather than seclude oneself at a neutral distance. Sure, there is a risk that this will initially influence their behaviour. But in time, and with responsible action on the camera team's part, the animals will soon settle and begin to go about their lives, completely ignoring the human presence and allowing a much deeper insight into who they are than otherwise possible.

As cameraman, you merge with the wind and the trees – you are a complete nonentity in the daily lives of those around you. And it is only then that you can start to record the essence of the beast that is the subject of your attentions. Being, too, almost a part of what is going on, the audience will come to believe they are also experiencing events first hand. As with the overwhelming sensory experience of an Imax or 3-D film, the idea is to stimulate all the senses, not only sight and sound, but subconsciously touch and smell as well.

These days it is not enough for a documentary to merely inform. Just as importantly it needs to entertain. Despite the noblest intention to inform and educate, without entertainment being an integral part of a wildlife film, the audience will soon switch off, skip to another channel, and the opportunity will be lost. It is only through satisfying, stimulating and challenging viewing that the international armchair audiences will support the conservation of our world's diminishing wildlife sanctuaries and the species they hold.

Possibly one of the biggest threats to come to all television is that of the present (and largely still pending) boom of the internet. Companies once safe and secure in their approach to programming are now having to reassess their thinking entirely. With the net streaming live images to worldwide audiences, this

KIM WOLHUTER & DALE HANCOCK

ABOVE AND OPPOSITE *What we like most about filming at night is that we have such creative control over the quality of our light – a luxury you do not have during the day.*

will become a truly informative, educational medium. Now, more than ever, the stories we make will have to be strong, dramatic, highly polished dramas – pieces of art – if they are going to survive.

After the initial three months of following her every move night and day, and witnessing almost every kill she made with the eventual hope that we would someday be in a fortunate enough position to film one of them, Tjellers started to change her tactics. We were constantly fighting a loosing battle against the intelligence of Tjellers, and leopards in general. No sooner had we worked out a possible strategy to capture one of her less predictable activities accurately on film than she turned the tables on us. We initially thought it would not be too much trouble to film one of her kills, as we were right there with her for nearly 30 different kills every month; but we were wrong. Trying to manoeuvre in behind her, close enough not to have our view obstructed by the dense Lowveld bush, and not to scare away her prey as she stalked in, was trying, to say the least.

KIM WOLHUTER & DALE HANCOCK

A further obstacle we had to conquer was the fact that, owing to our chosen style of nocturnal filming and the lighting equipment necessary, we sometimes had two vehicles to squeeze into position behind Tjellers without upsetting the applex-cart and scaring her prey. She soon learned that with us frantically trying to position our vehicles while she snuck up on her prey, she no longer had to be as cautious and silent a stalker as before. Although our presence and noise alerted the prey to the direction of her approach, she on the other hand had the advantage of being able to move in that much quicker than before, under cover of our vehicles' noises. If we thought our time was cut out for us over the initial three months when she used to sneak in slowly, now our situation was nearly impossible.

Once she had her sights set on her prey, following her by vehicle was out of the question. Unless her prey walked in her direction and almost stumbled over her in hiding (with us sitting silently in attendance nearby), we were not going to be successful. If our engines were running, she immediately closed the gap between herself and the hunted and was lost to sight. By the end of our project and after a little more than 300 hunts, we were only able to successfully capture

OVERLEAF *A common show down at Mala Mala. Hyaenas often hound leopards in the hope that the leopard might have, or lead them to something they can eat.*

PHOTOGRAPH: JAMES RAWDONS

Strangulation – the leopard's foremost technique for subduing larger prey.

four of them, from start to finish, on film. And those, frustratingly, only in the closing few months, as we became more adept at predicting her movements and setting up in advance of her.

This unintentional influence on one's subject's behaviour is a constant cause for concern for a wildlife film maker. There are many ways in which we could influence the outcome of a train of events, per chance or otherwise, but it is the responsibility of all reputable cameramen to minimize this wherever possible. The whole purpose of a documentary film is to document rather than influence. Wildlife, especially, is intricate and amazing enough without having to resort to unprofessional tactics to heighten the dramatic content of what one is recording.

If prepared to spend enough time and effort in the field, one's observations and the subsequent recorded material brought home will be peppered with more than enough spice and intrigue without having to resort to unethical attempts to achieve one's goals, as some might suggest. This is why we believe in spending at least 18 months with our subjects. Not only does this allow for a greater chance of witnessing interesting and unique behaviour, but it also allows us to develop an empathy with the specific characters of our films. This ultimately shows through in the end product. After a concrete story, real characters are the most important part of any 'docudrama'.

Wild animals are all potentially dangerous and should be respected as such. No matter how well acquainted one may become with them, there is no place for bravado. Even warthogs can pose a serious threat to the uninitiated. Their lower tusks are razor sharp, and if provoked or cornered an animal can slash open human flesh with a few well-timed lateral swipes of the head. Having said that though, in our first evening with the pregnant warthog in her hole, she allowed us to within touching distance and yet showed no negative reaction to our presence. Outside her burrow she would still warn us off from three to four metres, but somehow inside she had a sense of unchallenged security. She would sometimes stick her head so far through the neatly cut hole for our camera that we could hold her by the tusks without any response.

Growing up with us from birth, the piglets were completely at ease in our company. We were at their burrows before they came out and we stayed with them until they went below ground again, following them for the majority of this time on foot. Some would come and lie on our feet and rest a while before darting back to the group to join in the play. Likewise, the whole family group would gather under a bush to sleep for a few hours and were quite happy to let us lie with the group. It is moments like these that are the most rewarding, although the pigs usually 'hogged' all the shade.

Of course, trying to film both leopards and warthogs simultaneously over the two years would have been impossible. We had to separate the two. When operating with leopards it would mean an 18-hour day: out before sunset and back only the next morning after they had taken refuge from the heat of the day.

The warthogs were, therefore, a welcome change to this taxing routine, although we would still check on the leopards from time to time. Working a seven-day week, 12 weeks at a stretch, this can be quite draining, and on the rare occasion we would sleep in.

Such lapses came at a cost, however. For example, we had taken time out on New Year's day in 1995, only to learn to our frustration that we had missed an amazing warthog kill at one of our regular haunts close to Main Camp. Had we been out as usual that morning we would surely have been there to record it!

We were faced with one large moral dilemma whilst filming *Beauty and the Beasts*. If something were to happen that threatened the safety of one of our stars and we were in a position to prevent it, did we have the right to intervene, or was it maybe our obligation to do so? Many possibilities sprung to mind: hyaenas or lions threatening the lives of the cubs; death by drowning, or hypothermia in the warthog burrow; possible fatal injury from a snake bite or something similar; and so on.

Just the fact that the territories around the Tjellahanga River were so tightly packed and overcrowded with leopards, meant that there could be little hope for the survival of Two and Four. There simply wasn't anywhere they could move to on reaching adulthood. Unless they moved a long way off, or one of the dominant females in the area died for some reason, there simply wasn't any territory left to take. It was unlikely that even one of them would find a home in the immediate vicinity, let alone both of them. And without a home they would always be on the run, running from one female or another, battling to survive. Anything one of them killed would probably be taken from it by the rightful resident, and hunger and stress would soon begin to take its toll. Unpleasant as it was to accept, the future of the cubs was not bright, and in another year it was likely both would have vanished. Because we were closest to Four for obvious reasons, we hoped she would be the one to survive, if only one was to make it, but reason seemed to indicate that it would probably be Two, with her more cautious approach to life, who would pull through.

Then, almost as if we had tempted fate, Four contracted mange. Mange is most common in individuals already in poor condition. It is suggested that mites are present on most leopards, but only become virulent during periods of psychological stress. Four was starting to succumb to the pressures of her independent, adult life on the run. Once contracting mange it is unlikely an individual will ever recover. We had to make the choice: do we help her with modern-day medicine, or do we leave her to Nature's selective process? Usually we believe in letting Nature take its course, no matter how harsh it may be to stand by idly allowing some creature to suffer the compassionless verdict of nature.

We had already witnessed and recorded a number of such incidents during our filming, but none of these involved 'our' family. Not only were we very close to Four, but a vast amount of money had also been invested in this project. To

KIM WOLHUTER

The author with his vehicle of lights.

DALE HANCOCK

ABOVE *The cycle of life continues. These two unnamed cubs were borne to Tjellers in 1999.*

DALE HANCOCK

ABOVE *A tree squirrel.*

simply let her die of something so pointless when she was more valuable to us alive, not only from a filming point of view, but spiritually as well, we found ourselves, with little provocation, taking the proactive role. Darting her with Ivomac we gave her a second chance of life. Inevitably another leopard in the area would probably end up contracting mange and take her place, for the laws of Nature are relatively fixed. A way would be found to keep the areas carrying capacity for leopards at or below the necessary limit.

We were in 24-hour radio contact with all the operating vehicles and the three camps at Mala Mala, so we were able to take advantage of any sighting that was called in by them. We, in turn, would often allow the operators the benefit of our leopard sightings, but only if all the potential for filming for that day was over. We were obliged for the sake of the film to keep many of our sightings to ourselves, as too many vehicles continuously coming and going would likely impact negatively on filmable events of interest. When we would return to camp mid-morning for brunch after a full night's work with the leopards, the rangers would also quiz us in detail on what we had seen the night before. This, I am sure, was partially a genuine interest in all that we were seeing and recording on film, and partially a suspicion that we were seeing more than we were letting on; which we were. As our stories were not always water tight, they soon realized we were definitely not telling them everything of our nights' observations, but could never get us to admit it. In time they became wise to this and tried all manner of things to catch us out and find our sightings.

The rangers had started taking to following our fresh vehicle tracks off the road each morning in the hope that it would lead to Tjellers lying up somewhere for the day. As she had just given birth to her latest cub, Stevie, the race was also on to find her lair. Because we were able to follow her all night when she was most active, she had long since led us to the site where she had stashed her cub. We, too, were desperate for a shot of her moving her small charge from the lair and, therefore, were not going to tell the rangers just yet where exactly the site was. We were concerned we would miss the shot due to their presence and were thus keeping very mum.

On our last day of filming we drove some obvious tracks from and to one of the most well used roads on the property. We knew full well that the first vehicle out would see them and undoubtedly follow them in. As it happened, the property had at this stage been uncharacteristically very scarce of leopard sightings for some reason and the rangers were desperate for anything that might lead them to one. As predicted, the first vehicle to drive up the road stopped at the tracks for a time while the ranger contemplated their freshness and then promptly turned off the road. We, of course, were sitting a discrete distance away watching the whole saga. The tracks they were following, however, took

DALE HANCOCK

Tjellers moves through the thick woodland of her territory. To us she remains the most beautiful of all the leopards we have encountered.

them directly to a large marula tree and stopped. Facing them, in full view, up in the first fork of the tree was a leopard in all its splendour, printed on a high-gloss postcard.

Thankfully the guests thoroughly enjoyed the joke and, feeling guilty for our actions at their expense we duly gave them the site of the lair. That very morning, on the 2nd of February 1995, Tjellers moved her cub, performing perfectly for our camera and the ecstatic guests. A fitting end to two years of filming.

In the hustle and bustle of our everyday lives it is hard to believe there are such untempered, wild places left such as Mala Mala; where the leopard and the warthog are able to live out their sometimes simple, sometimes complicated lives. We count ourselves extremely fortunate to have been chosen to shoot such a documentary on the lives of just two of the animals that inhabit the untamed places of the African continent. But there are still many more stories to be told, and we intend to tell them.

PHOTOGRAPHERS' PROFILES

Peter Chadwick was born in Zimbabwe and turned an early interest in wildlife into a full-time occupation in nature conservation. His work has led him throughout southern Africa, and he has been involved in research projects in the Kruger National Park and the Kalahari Gemsbok National Park. He is now based with the KwaZulu-Natal Nature Conservation Service after having spent time working at Mala Mala Game Reserve. Chadwick's abiding interest in photography received international recognition when, in 1994, he won the Eric Hosking Award in the *BBC Wildlife*/British Gas 'Wildlife Photographer of the Year' competition, for his portfolio on Kalahari wildlife. His photographic work has also been widely published in magazines and books, both locally and internationally.

Pieter Dros has been a ranger and manager at Mala Mala Game Reserve since 1995. His interest in photography developed while at Mala Mala, where he has made use of the endless opportunities the Lowveld wildlife presents to hone his skills. Originally from a cattle-farming background in the Northern Province, his love for the outdoors was instilled at a young age. After his schooling in Pretoria his family relocated to the Cape and he enrolled at the University of Stellenbosch, where he obtained a Bachelor's Degree in economics. Dros soon realised economics was not for him and he subsequently enrolled at the Port Elizabeth Technikon, Saasveld Campus, where he completed his National Diploma in Nature Conservation. A year of practical training in the Timbavati Private Nature Reserve nurtured his fascination for the bush and its wildlife.

Chris Daphne was born in 1966 and grew up in the Eastern Cape. After leaving school he spent eight years years at University of Natal, Pietermaritzburg, where he completed his M.Sc. in Grassland Science. From university he went directly to Mala Mala Game Reserve with the intention of staying only a year or so as a game ranger. Seven years later he is still at Mala Mala. Although photography is not his profession, it has become a major hobby.

Richard du Toit grew up on a farm near Pietermartizburg and as a young boy was a very keen bird-watcher. He completed a B.Sc. (Hons) degree at the University of Natal (Pietermaritzburg), majoring in zoology and entomology, and then began his working career as a ranger at Mala Mala Game Reserve. In 1995 he won first place in the 'mammals behaviour' category in the internationally renowned *BBC Wildlife*/British Gas 'Wildlife Photographer of the Year' competition. This prompted him to realise his life-long dream of becoming a wildlife photographer. Du Toit now works full-time as a freelance photographer, and travels widely in southern Africa in pursuit of images of nature and wildlife taken in wild and free conditions. His photographs have been widely published throughout the world in calendars, books, journals and magazines. Magazines he has worked with include *GEO*, *Sierra Club* magazine, *BBC Wildlife*, *Africa – Environment & Wildlife* and *Africa – Birds & Birding*. Du Toit is currently working on several illustrated books.

Quinton Hadden was born in Johannesburg and as a young boy was fortunate enough to spend a lot of time at Mashatu Game Reserve, where his love and respect for the bush developed. In 1997 he graduated from the University of Nottingham with a B.Sc. (Hons) degree in environmental biology. Hadden then returned to South Africa, where he started working for Mala Mala Game Reserve as a ranger, a position he continues to hold. Although he won awards at school for photography, Hadden's interest really started growing at Mala Mala, where exposure to incredible subject matter and experienced photographers provided the opportunity to develop his expertise.

Nils Kure studied zoology before joining Mala Mala Game Reserve as a ranger in 1988. He is not specifically interested in photography, but has pursued it on account of the opportunities available. He currently manages Main Camp at Mala Mala.

Graham Mitchell-Innes was born and raised on a farm in KwaZulu-Natal. Living on a farm nurtured a love for the wild. After completing an agricultural management degree, he joined Mala Mala Game Reserve as a game ranger, where his interest in photography burgeoned.

Peter Nicholson grew up on a farm in KwaZulu-Natal where he developed a love of wildlife. He went on to study for a B.Sc. degree. After working in the Okavango Delta, he spent a year at Phinda Resource Reserve. It was here that his interest in wildlife photography started, but it was only when he moved to the Sabi Sand Game Reserve that it became a passion. Nicholson is currently working in the travel industry in Johannesburg.

James Rawdon was born in the United Kingdom, but immigrated to South Africa at a very early age. He immediately took an immense interest in nature, regularly visiting the wildlife areas of southern Africa. After school, his interest in photography first took root. After completing a B.Sc. degree he started as a game ranger at Mala Mala, remaining there for three-and-a-half years. Rawdon describes his time at Mala Mala as an unforgettable experience, especially as he had the privilege of spending many hours with the resident leopards. He is currently a camp manager in the Okavango Delta.

Rowan Stretton's interest in wildlife photography began in 1997 while working in the Kalahari Gemsbok National Park. He is also a very keen artist and started photography primarily to provide a source for his artwork. After obtaining his National Diploma in Conservation, he became a ranger at Mala Mala where he takes full advantage of the wildlife photographic opportunities. Stretton regards himself as an aspiring amateur, and photography as a hobby he will enjoy for the rest of his life.

Jamie Thom began taking photographs at the age of 17 under the guidance of his father. While studying mechanical engineering and working in the vehicle manufacturing industry he got to know his neighbours, who were keen game-viewers and photographers. He became interested immediately, making regular trips to the Kruger National Park. Wildlife and photography soon became more important than engineering and he began to pursue his new interests. He was accepted at Mala Mala where he trained to be a ranger and has been there for three years. Thom has won numerous awards for his photography, including overall winner of the *BBC Wildlife*/British Gas 'Wildlife Photographer of the Year' award in 1999. He recently collaborated on a book on Mala Mala: *Pathway to an African Eden.*

Kim Wolhuter grew up in the Kruger National Park where his father, Henry, was senior ranger. After graduating, his interests turned to photographing and filming wildlife and, as cameraman for Richard Goss, he worked on such acclaimed films as *The Sisterhood, Strandwolf, Wild Horses of the Namib*, and *Beauty and the Beasts.* Since 1995 he has worked independently, producing and shooting his own films: *Black Jack – High Stakes* and *Impala – Basic Instincts*, for Survival Anglia Ltd. Presently he is producing a film on leopards at Mala Mala. He has filmed for National Geographic Television, BBC Natural History Unit and Survival Anglia, amongst others. His awards include the 1997 SA Society of Cinematographers 'Visible Spectrum' Award for cinematography, winner of the 1998 AGFA competition and, also in 1998, he received a 'highly commended' in the *BBC Wildlife*/British Gas 'Wildlife Photographer of the Year' awards.

James Wakelin, naturalist and photographer, was born in 1972 in Harding. While completing his military service in the Kruger National Park, his interest in photography began to develop. Later, as a ranger at Mala Mala, Wakelin gained first-class experience in wildlife photography. He currently works for the KwaZulu-Natal Nature Conservation Service, where he is primarily involved in the field of biodiversity conservation.

PHOTOGRAPH: NILS KURE